Giorgione

Giorgione

Arnoldo Mondadori Arte

Texts by Stefano Zuffi

Translation by David Stanton

Table of Contents

Giorgione

In the history of art the case of Giorgione is truly unique, almost paradoxical. We know very little about the artist, who was active in Venice at the height of the Renaissance, a period in which information about painters was generally plentiful; the paintings attributed to him with certainty, which were referred to by the oldest sources, are few and far between. Yet over four centuries Giorgione's fame and glory have never been in doubt.

While his career is an important landmark in the development of Italian art at the beginning of the sixteenth century, he is one of the most renowned and well-loved painters of all time. By embroidering fanciful tales around the meagre details of his life the figure of a romantic hero has been constructed—a passionate youth who died when he was just over thirty, who with his brushwork conjured up the mellow atmosphere of the Venetian landscape, the idyllic pastoral life and a world of young people in love, lute players and beautiful maidens. A critical study of Giorgione's art and the attempt to reconstruct his *oeuvre*—not an easy task due to his close collaboration with other painters of his time, especially Sebastiano del Piombo and Titian—have often been hindered by a literary and decidedly romantic interpretation of the artist's personality.

Apart from the ruined, almost indecipherable, frescoes of the Fondaco dei Tedeschi, there are only four paintings which can be accepted unquestionably as being by Giorgione—the *Tempest* (Plates 17, 18), the *Three Philosophers* (Plates 19, 20), the *Sleeping Venus* (Plates, 21, 22), and the *Castelfranco Altarpiece* (Plates 13-15). Are these works, two of which are not completely by the artist, enough to create a myth? The answer has to be an affirmative one, not only because of the spontaneous charm that inspires their moving poetic sentiment or the fascinating yet evasive figure of the artist. In fact, Giorgione is the central and decisive link in the chain which extends from Giovanni Bellini to Titian. In the early years of the sixteenth century, thanks to these major Venetian painters, Italian painting experienced a notable evolution in technique and composition which aimed at an "atmospheric" rendering of the image.

Giorgione was not a romantic lover of nature,

but rather an artist who was engaged in avant-garde research. By following in Giovanni Bellini's footsteps with total conviction, he formulated a personal and fully-conscious definition of "tonality." He painted without insisting overmuch on careful drawing, aiming rather to depict the delicate chiaroscuros of the various colour tones with painterly rather than linear means. This solution, which he subjected to continuous verification by observing the real world, was not only adopted for landscape, but also for human figures, which appear to be bathed in warm luminosity with delicately softened outlines.

Moreover, an important innovation was the use of "coloured shadows"—Giorgione obtained the colour of the area in shadow of, for example, drapery not by simply mixing in black or by painting over a dark glaze to tone down the area in the light, but by selecting a new, more intense colour. This technique was destined to have a large following up to the last century, when it was adopted with great enthusiasm by the Impressionists. The quiet and serene themes, the peaceful atmosphere of the Venetian hills, the nicely calculated alternation between suffused light and soft shadows bring to mind an eternal untroubled idyll. But this was only a part of Giorgione's visual poetry. In reality, especially in the later works, a vein of melancholy and apprehension, at times even drama, crept in.

For this reason it is not possible to sustain the stereotype of Giorgione engrossed in the poetic vision of a legend, the contented bard of a mythical golden age, who, as Vasari put it "took continuous delight in the affairs of love, and was extremely fond of the music of the lute, so much so that he played and sang really divinely." On the contrary, his brief career as an artist, brought to an untimely end by the plague of 1510, must be interpreted in the context of the intense and inspired relationship he enjoyed with the culture and traditions of the Republic of Venice at a significant turning point in the history of art.

The Young Giorgione and Venetian Culture in the Early Sixteenth Century

There is a complete lack of documents which registered Giorgione's surname and the place and date of his birth. The oldest sources are sometimes contradictory, but they allow us to establish that the artist was born in about 1477 or 1478, in the province of Treviso, probably in Castelfranco or, perhaps, in the nearby village of Vedelago. He was first called "Giorgione" (literally "Big George") by Paolo Pino in *Dialogo della Pittura* (1548); previously he had simply been referred to as "Zorzi" or "Zorzo da Castelfranco" in Veneto dialect. Now that the story that he was a member of the Barbarelli family (perhaps as an illegitimate son) has been given the lie, the painter's origins remain unknown—in any case they were "obscure" for Vasari. He learned to paint in Venice, but there is no record of the name of the teacher with whom he completed his apprenticeship, about which we can, therefore, only surmise.

Despite all these doubts, one thing is certain—when Giorgione was about twenty years old he came to Venice and was immediately introduced into the cultural circles of the aristocracy and, at the same time, he clearly managed to keep very up-to-date on artistic matters. Around 1500 the fortunes of the Republic of St. Mark were at a high point. In contrast with the other Italian states, which had begun to suffer severe attacks from abroad, its possessions in the Adriatic, the Aegean and the Eastern Mediterranean had reached their maximum extent. The efficient trading network, which was sustained by a perfect administrative set-up and an excellent diplomatic service, was able to withstand the wasteful nepotism of Doge Agostino Barbarigo, who was succeeded in 1501 by Leonardo Loredan.

At the end of the fifteenth century Queen Caterina Cornaro ceded the island of Cyprus to the Venetian Republic, receiving in exchange the fief of Asolo (not far from Castelfranco). Here she fostered a cultivated group of literati and artists, among whom the most noteworthy was the poet and linguist Pietro Bembo, whose name has on occasion been linked with the cultural circles frequented by Giorgione. Besides its maritime possessions, Venice consolidated its *terraferma* empire, which extended from the River Adda in the west (with Bergamo, Brescia and Crema) to Veneto and Friuli in the east and Romagna in the south. At the historic university of Padua there were animated Venetian cultural circles, which were also frequented by Giorgione's patrons. The diffusion of printing, with refined compact editions by Aldo Manunzio, favoured literary activity.

These events of the last decade of the fifteenth century took place against the background of the sensational discoveries of new continents, which allowed the opening up of trading routes across the Atlantic to the New World or towards the East with the circumnavigation of Africa. Spain and Portugal lost no time in taking advantage of the situation, thereby creating further problems for the economies of the Mediterranean countries, already facing the growing Turkish threat.

The young Venetian patricians, who had already realised the extent of the risk to sea trade, discovered an alternative economic activity in agriculture, and financed ambitious land reclamation schemes, above all in the Po Delta and the area around Padua. The patricians' investment in the exploitation of the land was the first step towards the "civilisation of villas" so typical of the culture and landscape of Veneto.

This economic and cultural situation was reflected in the tastes of the artists and their patrons, above all when Giovanni Bellini carried out his patient and poetic research into the representation of atmospheric effects. Despite the local variations within an enormous output, painting in Veneto in the early sixteenth century was totally taken up with the light and colour of landscape, both in the form of panoramas of the countryside and urban views.

Venetian architecture, which was gradually abandoning delicate Gothic tracery, was now making its acquaintance with the calmer rhythms and curvilinear elegance of Mauro Codussi, while various sculptors from Lombardy—such as Andrea Bregno and the Lombardo family—decorated both interiors and exteriors with refined bas-reliefs. The pictorial record of this renewed Venice was entrusted to a series of vast narrative paintings with episodes set in the city itself, a genre in which Giovanni Bellini and Vittore Carpaccio excelled.

Also in the province of Treviso, where Castelfranco is situated, the theme of the presence of nature in art was given a great deal of importance, even though details were depicted with clear-cut precision, which seemed to be the contrary of Giorgione's soft outlines. Cima da Conegliano was the most noteworthy painter from the Treviso area at the beginning of the sixteenth century; often in the backgrounds of his paintings he depicted the sharply-defined landscape of the hills near the River Piave, based on the direct observation of reality. The city and the province of Treviso were the scene of intense artistic activity, thanks to Bishop Bernardo de' Rossi, the patron and "discoverer" of Lorenzo Lotto, who was just a little younger than Giorgione. It is possible that, before moving to Venice, the young artist from Castelfranco had learnt the rudiments of painting from local artists, such as Pier Maria Pennacchi or Gerolamo da Treviso.

It was probable that these first steps allowed Giorgione to be immediately introduced into Venetian artistic circles and make contact with Giovanni Bellini, but he was at the same time open to other influences. In Giorgione's early work it is possible to observe evident signs of the arrival in Venice, around 1500, of a variety of major painters such as Dürer, Leonardo and Bosch, as well as an interest in classicism, which was central Italian in taste, fostered in Bologna and Mantua by the delicately graceful Francesco Francia and Lorenzo Costa. Not so much a pupil of a single master, during his early artistic education Giorgione was receptive to various new influences, as was the case with his contemporary, Raphael.

Giorgione's total output was concentrated in little more than ten years, but from his earliest works he was accustomed to working with other painters, which makes it even more difficult to attribute and date so many of them. An early example is constituted by the two paintings in the Galleria degli Uffizi in Florence—the *Trial of Moses* and the *Judgement of Solomon* (Plates 1-3). Here, in compositions that are still fifteenth century in style, a number of figures and many details of the landscape showing the delicate hand of the young Giorgione are noticeable, while other groups of figures are by another artist, perhaps from Ferrara.

The structure of the small but refined *Madonna with Saint Catherine and Saint John the Baptist* in the Accademia in Venice (Plate 5) is usually considered to be a trial run for Giorgione's early output in Venice, even though some critics consider it to be painted by Sebastiano del Piombo using a composition by Giorgione as a basis.

The early work by Sebastiano Luciani (he only assumed the nickname of "del Piombo" in 1531, after having obtained a much desired office from Pope Clement VII, that is to say keeper of the papal seals, which were made of lead—"piombo" in Italian) was closely linked with that of Giorgione. According to the Venetian collector and connoisseur Marcantonio Michiel—who left invaluable information about the original purchasers of a number of Giorgione's paintings—Sebastiano even collaborated in the painting of the *Three Philosophers* (Plates 19, 20). The attribution of works such as *Christ and the Audulteress* (Art Gallery, Glasgow) and the *Shepherd with a Flute* (Galleria di Capodimonte, Naples) is still open to debate—however they could be ascribed to Sebastiano.

In the first five years of the sixteenth century, with the *Judith* in the Hermitage Museum in Leningrad, Giorgione tried his hand at a figure of large dimensions, thus verifying the application of tonality to obtain effects of wistful grace. It should be mentioned that the landscape seems to be inspired by the Umbrian or Tuscan countryside rather than that of Veneto; in fact in the past the painting was thought to be by Raphael. Once this untenable theory had been put aside, the Leningrad *Judith* became one of the few works about which scholars are in total agreement, and this also regards the early dating, while for many of the later paintings there are still doubts concerning their attributions.

The favourite theme of Giorgione and his patrons in this period seems to have been the Nativity or the Madonna and Child in a landscape. The version which contains the greatest number of figures is the *Adoration of the Magi* (Plate 8) in the National Gallery in London. In this fairly small painting, which is an elongated rectangle in shape, Giorgione experimented with colours that are certainly vivid (the golden colour of Joseph's mantle is somewhat unusual), but which harmonise in the carefully arranged softening of the outlines. Simpler, but no less graceful, is the *Holy Family* in the National Gallery of Art in Washington (Plate 7), known as the "*Benson Madonna*" from the name of the last owner. The loose folds of the Virgin's cloak, spread out on the stony ground bring to mind Flemish art, as does the small *Madonna and Child* in the Hermitage, set in mountain scenery (Plate 12).

The *Virgin and Child with Venice Behind* (also known as the *Madonna Reading* or the *Tallard Madonna*) in the Ashmolean Museum in Oxford (Plates 10, 11), with a more monumental compositional structure, poses a subtle problem, linked to the representation of the urban landscape. The window in the background opens onto an unmistakable view of the Piazzetta di San Marco, where a veiled and decidedly sketchy rendering of the Doge's Palace and other buildings has given rise to the theory that the painting was unfinished, unless it was, in fact, an original study of Leonardo's technique.

The most important of this group of paintings is the *Adoration of the Shepherds*, known as the "*Allendale Nativity*," in the National Gallery of Art in Washington, which can be considered to be the masterpiece of Giorgione's early years, (Plate 9). The rarefied atmosphere of silent meditation suggests the possible influence of the contemporary Umbrian painting of Perugino and Pinturicchio, but the domination of natural elements—depicted in great detail and, in particular, with the barely perceptible diffusion of light—is a sign of a new poetic and painterly sentiment. Giorgione had now acquired a technique which, in effect, allowed him to eliminate precisely drawn outlines. Remarkable proof of this is to be found in the *Frieze with Instruments of the Liberal Arts*, a monochrome painting in a room of the Casa Pellizzari in Castelfranco, which is now known as the "Casa del Giorgione" (Plate 4).

From the Castelfranco Altarpiece to the Frescoes of the Fondaco dei Tedeschi—The Masterpieces of Giorgione's Mature Period

The *Castelfranco Altarpiece* (Plates 13-15) marked the midway point of Giorgione's artistic career. Painted for *condottiere* Tuzio Costanzo's chapel in the cathedral of his home town, it was the artist's only painting intended for a church. Executed around 1504 or 1505, while Giovanni Bellini was painting the great *San Zaccaria Altarpiece* in Venice, Giorgione's *Enthroned Madonna with Saint Liberale and Saint Francis* did not distance itself from the traditional model of the *sacra conversazione*, with the enthroned Madonna placed between the saints in a pyramidal spatial structure. The figure of Saint Francis was even taken from the "old" *San Giobbe Altarpiece* by Giovanni Bellini. The young painter courageously chose, therefore, to abandon the architectonic delineation of forms in order to allow the balmy atmosphere of the landscape to circulate between the figures, with tones of light and colour in perfect harmony. The natural effect is favoured by the unusual compositional elements (the parapet behind the figures), the iconographic innovations (the Madonna's green robe) and the technical experimentation (the colours are made up of superimposed glazes, without preliminary drawing). In the same period Giorgione executed a number of portraits, some of them half-length, but as with the rest of his output, the attribution of these paintings raises a lot of doubts. In this case, however, it is possible to refer to an authentic inscription, which mentions both the painter and the date (1st July 1506) of the female portrait known as *Laura* in the Kunsthistorisches Museum in Vienna (Plate 16); the same woman appears as the female nude in the *Tempest* (Plates 17, 18). The two similar small paintings, *Young Man Holding an Arrow* (Kunsthistorisches Museum, Vienna) and *Shepherd with a Flute* (Royal Collections, Hampton Court), with their vaguely Leonardesque associations, are contemporary.

The *Tempest* (Accademia, Venice; Plates 17, 18) is the most well-known and enigmatic of Giorgione's paintings. Even his contemporaries were not able to fathom out the theme, thus giving rise to the myth of the artist who painted without a subject, or who produced works for a narrow circle of intellectuals sharing a common passion for esoteric literature. Using one of these publications (the *Hypnerotomachia Poliphili*) as a basis, attempts have been made, not always with great success, to interpret various works by Giorgione. A recent endeavour has seen in the *Tempest* a representation of the expulsion of Adam and Eve from paradise, but, whatever its significance may be, the painting fully expresses the charm of nature in a moment of intense sensuousness.

A return to the contemplation of landscape, but with greater emphasis than in the calm idylls of his early years, can be noted in Giorgione's *Aeneas and Anchises in the Underworld* in the National Gallery in London and the *Three Philosophers* (Plates 19, 20) in Vienna.

Regarding the latter painting, it has been credibly suggested that it depicts the three Magi on their journey to Bethlehem. Giorgione used this as a pretext for developing the theme, of which the culture of Veneto of the early sixteenth century was so fond, of the three ages of man, and above all for a deeper study of the presence of the human figure in a landscape, in which he developed new psychological nuances. The colours of the robes of the three figures are extremely vivid, but once again the hues seem to blend together in the overall luminosity.

By this time, the young painter was one of the most respected painters in Venice. Between 1507 and 1508 he executed a painting (now lost) for the Doge's Palace, and this official commission was followed in 1508 by the prestigious task of decorating the Fondaco dei Tedeschi, which had been rebuilt following a fire.

Giorgione was responsible for the façade fronting onto the Grand Canal, leaving to his up-and-coming collaborator, Titian, the side facing the Mercerie.

The frescoes had evidently been completed by 8 November 1508, when Giorgione, who was not satisfied with the payment, submitted the work to a committee of experts, presided over by Giovanni Bellini and consisting of Vittore Carpaccio, Lazzaro Bastiani and Vittore di Matteo. The frescoes have nearly all been lost and the only record is through a number of eighteenth century engravings and in the figure of the *Nude* in the Galleria Franchetti (Plate 23), which has been reduced to an almost undecipherable remnant. Yet these limited remains are sufficient to throw light on the notable difference in style between Giorgione and the young and extremely dynamic Titian.

It is often said that Titian was Giorgione's "pupil," but in fact he became part of Giorgione's retinue when he had already completed his artistic education. While in some cases it is impossible to distinguish between the style of the two artists, from his earliest works Titian revealed a taste for drama which could never be confused with Giorgione's more delicate sensibility. Perhaps it was due to the rivalry with Titian that between November 1508—when he completed the Fondaco frescoes—and November 1510—when he died—that Giorgione painted works in which his youthful serenity gave way to a more meditative, at times even bitter, atmosphere.

The Last Works—From Giorgione to the Giorgionesques

The *Portrait of an Old Lady* (Plate 28), in the Accademia in Venice, among the few certain works by Giorgione, is perhaps the most disconcerting of his paintings. The artist who is always described in breathlessly poetic terms produced here a sombre and disenchanted image of the way beauty fades with the passing of time. The elderly woman, in whose aged features it is possible to discern the shadow of irrevocably lost charms, holds a sign with the inscription "*col tempo*" ("with time") and stares at the spectator with an expression of hopelessness.

It is possible, therefore, to speak of an allegorical painting, as in the case of the *Three Ages of Man* or *Concert* in the Galleria Palatina, Palazzo Pitti in Florence (Plates 36, 37). Of the various versions of this theme—sometimes represented in the form of a concert—this is the one which is most probably by Giorgione. Also the portraits, such as the *Portrait of a Young Man* (also known as the *Giustiniani Portrait*) at the Staatliche Museen in Berlin (Plate 24) and the *Terris Portrait* in the San Diego Museum, once the usual problems of attribution have been overcome, display a similar meditative attitude which is intensely introspective. The extremely delicate handling of the paint accentuates the subtly penetrating psychology of the sitters. Vasari reported the presence of a *Self-Portrait as David*, now with the lower part missing, in the Herzog Anton Ulrich Museum in Brunswick (Plate 25). Once again the supposed artist-poet of nature offered a decidedly non-idyllic image, but with fascinating and pathetically human content.

Other Venetian portraits, which can be dated around 1510, have a similar vein of romantic nostalgia, depicted with noble poses. Among these is the *Portrait of a Young Man* in the Szépmüvészeti Museum in Budapest, the portrait which is known as the *Gattamelata* in the Uffizi (Plates 33, 34) and the *Double Portrait* (at least as far as the figure in the foreground is concerned) in the Museo di Palazzo Venezia in Rome (Plate 29). In all these cases the attribution to Giorgione is not accepted by many scholars, even though the sentimental tone and the distinctive handling of the paint definitely suggest the circle of followers of Giorgione, who was then about thirty years old. In fact it is incorrect to use the term "workshop" in connection with Giorgione—rather there was a large group of artists who adopted his style and iconography.

There was very close collaboration between these artists—Giorgione himself wrote that he was a *cholega* ("colleague" in Venetian dialect) of Vincenzo Catena on the back of the *Laura* (Plate 16), in Vienna. In a number of paintings, including some important ones, the impression is given that several artists were working together, perhaps in competition with one other. This is the case with the *Concert* in the Galleria Palatina, Palazzo Pitti in Florence (Plates 36, 37), where it is possible that Giorgione may have prepared the original composition. The man at the spinet, in the centre, is certainly by Titian, while the other two figures are by anonymous Giorgionesque painters. The phenomenon of the Giorgionesques was very extensive and influenced the taste of the Venetian collectors to the extent that more than a century after the artist's death the producers of false Giorgiones were still doing a roaring trade. The painters who first followed in Giorgione's innovatory footsteps, besides the case of Sebastiano del Piombo which has already been mentioned, were above all young artists from the *terraferma* who had moved to Venice. They included Jacopo Palma il Vecchio, Andrea Previtali and Bernardino Licinio from Bergamo, Paris Bordon and Domenico Mancini from Treviso and Giulio Campagnola from Padua—the latter artist's engravings were of great importance in making Giorgionesque compositions and motifs known to the public.

But the strongest personality of all was certainly that of Titian, who came to Venice as an adolescent from Pieve di Cadore around 1500. In 1508 he worked with Giorgione on the Fondaco dei Tedeschi frescoes, and in the following years, despite stylistic differences, he became a total master of the artist's style, sowing disconcertion among the experts. Vasari admitted quite frankly that he had great difficulty in distinguishing Titian's hand from that of Giorgione in portraits and other paintings, even when some of these were among the most famous paintings in Venice, for instance the *Christ Carrying the Cross* in the Scuola Grande di San Rocco in Venice (Plate 35).

The old sources, backed up by X-ray analysis, bear witness to Titian's involvement in the completion of Giorgione's last masterpiece, the *Sleeping Venus* in the Gemäldegalerie in Dresden (Plates 21, 22), which had perhaps been left unfinished as a result of the artist's sudden death at the end of October 1510, during a serious epidemic of plague. The episode was described by Vasari as follows: "... he fell in love with a lady, and their delight in their amours knew no bounds. Now it came to pass that she caught the plague. Not being aware of this, Giorgione continued to frequent her as he habitually did, thus she infected him with the disease, so that in a short space of time ... he passed away." In the Dresden *Sleeping Venus* we find Giorgione's typical contemplative spirit in the depiction of the calm beauty of a girl asleep, which is reflected in the very rhythm of the hills and the surrounding vegetation, while the inclusion of the brilliant expanse of white drapery is almost certainly the work of Titian.

In this case scholars almost unanimously accept the distinction between the work of the two artists, but the disagreements over Titian and Giorgione have not yet been resolved as far as other painting are concerned, and perhaps they never will be. These works include the celebrated *Fête Champêtre* in the Louvre in Paris (Plate 32) and the *Virgin and Child with Saint Anthony and Saint Roch* in the Prado in Madrid (Plates 30, 31).

The Legacy

Giorgione's early death, at an age of about thirty-two, provoked two effects. On the one hand it surrounded the artist's figure with an aura of unhappy legend, and on the other hand it favoured the phenomenon of the Giorgionesque painters. The painter from Castelfranco was one of the few artists whose fame has never declined. But the definition of his oeuvre is fraught with difficulties and doubts, which are also linked to the production of replicas by his contemporaries and forgeries in the seventeenth century—in this regard the Giorgionesque paintings by Pietro Muttoni are proverbial. These doubtful attributions were backed up by increasingly imaginative historical reconstructions, like those by Carlo Ridolfi.

Little by little, during the sixteenth century, Titian's art abandoned its original tenets in order to give Giorgione's tonality unexpected expressive force. Thus there was the evolution from painting based on delicate, barely perceptible passages of light to a use of colour involving bold, sweeping brushwork. The reference to the painting of the early sixteenth century on the part of artists such as the Brescian Savoldo was taken by the painters of the High and Late Renaissance to be a study of the effects of chiaroscuro. In the light of this it is possible to comprehend the words of a Roman painter who, at the beginning of the seventeenth century considered Caravaggio to be a "new Giorgione."

While the seventeenth and eighteenth centuries are the ones in which the myth of Giorgione was built up, during the nineteenth century, a more precise study of the artist was finally initiated.

At the end of the last century, Giorgione once became again a model for painters, so that, for example, the *Fête Champêtre* in the Louvre (Plate 32) was carefully studied by Manet. The Impressionists continued the basic characteristics of tonality, interpretating it in the light of the scientific discoveries in the field of photography, in particular the way the image was formed on the plate.

Towards the end of the last century with great courage two Italian scholars, Cavalcaselle and Morelli, drastically reduced Giorgione's *oeuvre* to a few certain paintings, but other scholars have preferred to continue to attribute a very large number of works to the artist. Consequently, despite invaluable research by scholars such as Berenson, Gronau Lionello and Adolfo Venturi, Longhi and Fiocco and Morassi, there is still no unanimous agreement. Besides, the doubts regard not only works of secondary importance, but also true masterpieces.

In 1955 a major exhibition in Venice was an occasion for scholars to compare notes and for the public to become familiar with his works. The choice of works was intentionally anything but selective. While the exhibition had the merit of offering for the first time an all-round study of the phenomenon of the Giorgionesques, the number of paintings presented as authentic Giorgiones was probably excessive.

Later studies by Pallucchini, Coletti, Morassi and Zampetti and the famous research by Settis into the interpretation of the *Tempest* (Plates 17, 18) and the *Three Philosophers* (Plates 19, 20) were the prelude to two conferences in 1978—fifth centenary of the presumed date of Giorgione's birth. Here the certainties and the areas of debate in research into Giorgione's painting were restated, while attention was focused on the need for a more attentive study of Venetian culture of the early sixteenth century.

Anthology of Comments

Giorgione had seen a number of works by Leonardo which were shaded off in the manner of smoke and painted, as has been said, in extremely dark colours. And this manner pleased him greatly, so that while he was alive he always took it to be his model, and in his oil painting he imitated it very much. Taking a great liking to this way of working, he chose to paint the most beautiful and various things that he came across. He gave such a benign spirit to nature, that both in oil painting and frescoes he created many vivid images and other things which were delicate, harmonious and shaded off in dark colours, which was the reason why many of those who were excellent painters at that time declared that he had been born to put life into his figures and to imitate the bloom of the living flesh more than anyone else who had ever painted, not only in Venice, but also anywhere else.
(G. Vasari, *Le Vite de' più eccellenti pittori, scultori ed architettori*, 1568)

At the same time that Florence became famous thanks to to the works of Leonardo, because of the excellence of Giorgione from Castelfranco near Treviso the name of Venice gained new glory.
(R. Borghini, *Il Riposo*, 1584)

In painting he found that the impasto of the brush was more delicate than it had ever been before. And it must be said that the brushwork was flesh mixed with blood, but in such a harmonious and easy manner that it is no longer possible to talk about pictorial artifice, but rather the truth of Nature. This is because in the shading off of the outlines (which even caused Nature itself to marvel), in the handling of light colours and half-tones, in the application of ruddy tints and modelling of the areas of colour he created such wonderful and convincing harmony that it must be described as painted Nature, or indeed painting which had become Nature itself. The ideas of this painter were all momentous, of considerable maturity and worthy of the greatest respect. In fact, this was reflected in his name, Giorgione [literally "Big George"], and for this reason his talent created solemn figures wearing large hats, adorned with strange plumes, dressed in an old-fashioned manner, with blous-

es seen under heavy jackets which are cut with puffed sleeves, and dragoons in the style of Giovanni Bellini, but more handsomely painted. And his draperies were of silk, velvet, damask and satin with wide ribs and other figures wore shining armour, and it was the true representation of human deeds.
(M. Boschini, *Le ricche minere della pittura veneziana*, 1674)

Hardly had he apprehended the excellent principles, when he began to feel the magnitude of his genius, brimming over with youthful ardour and a certain natural violence, for which reason he came forth in great haste from his earlier timorousness and imbued his figures with the vividness which they had lacked up to that time... Colour acquired full flavour in his hands, which were able to imitate the bloom of living flesh to perfection... The strength and fullness which Giorgione was able to give to his figures did not prevent his painting, as was the case with other Painters, from creating beauty, boldness and ruddy tinted flesh which practically glowed with life.
(A.M. Zanetti, *Della pittura veneziana*, 1771)

Guided by an inexorable desire to discover what he was capable of, he scorned that pettiness which was yet to be overcome. In its place he substituted a degree of freedom, almost nonchalance, in which the highest point of art lies. He could be considered to be the inventor of this genre of painting, since no one before him had been able to handle the brush so resolutely, nor were they so able to model through areas of colour or astound the viewer from afar. He continued then to improve his manner, softening the outlines and taking a new approach to foreshortening, with a more vivid depiction of faces and gestures, a more careful selection of the draperies and other accessories, a more natural and delicate gradation from one colour to another and, lastly, a stronger and much more effective use of chiaroscuro.
(L. Lanzi, *Storia pittorica dell'Italia*, 1795-1796)

His original and eminently poetic talent radiates such a pure light, while his simple and straightforward artistic flair addresses us with such strength and appeal, that whosoever pays heed to it but once will never forget it.
(G. Morelli, *Le opera dei Maestri italiani*, 1880)

Indeed it would be difficult to say anything more about Giorgione than this: that his works are a crystal clear mirror of the Renaissance at its highest point.
(B. Berenson, *The Venetian Painters of the Renaissance*, New York, London, 1894)

He appears as a myth rather than as a man. On this earth no poet's destiny is comparable with his. Nothing, or almost nothing, is known about him, and some go as far as to deny that he ever existed. His name is not inscribed on any of his works; there are those who do not ascribe any paintings to him with certainty. Yet the whole of Venetian art seemed to have been fired with enthusiasm by his revelation.
(G. D'Annunzio, *Il Fuoco*, 1898)

Starting from the style of painters such as Bellini and Carpaccio, he set off in various directions, towards linear refinement as well as towards a painterly touch, achieving in the space of a few years what Venetian painting had done in a century, extemporizing everything as and when necessary, with the exception of that guiding principle, his perceptiveness. Let it not be said either that Giorgione was more of a poet than a painter; on the contrary it was precisely because he was more of a poet than the others that he revolutionised painting and created a new vision of the world. Nor is it surprising if a young man aged between twenty-five and thirty, while achieving this prodigy, should have had his moments of uncertainty, backsliding, sudden impulse and weariness.
(L. Venturi, *Giorgione*, 1954)

Giorgione will always be the genius who, having perceived the vital harmony of nature, did not approach it from a one-sided point of view, but rather from a universal one. For Giorgione man lived in the natural environment, indeed he was part of it. The division between man and nature in the fifteenth century had been overcome. Giorgione had narrated all this in a new manner of painting, in which colour with all its brilliant

variations and its infinite possibilities assumed a role of fundamental importance, because it is precisely with this means that the artist could create his poetic vision. The clear-cut outlines disappeared, everything became softer and permeated with light.
This light, which seemed to radiate from the objects themselves, was inconstant, unstable and wavering like human sentiment itself.
(P. Zampetti, introduction to *Giorgione e i giorgioneschi*, exhibition catalogue, Venice 1955)

[In the *Adoration of the Magi* in the National Gallery, London] there is a contrast that is deliberate: on one side the Holy Family, tranquilly seated with the ox and the ass, simple of form but the more majestic in their solidity, the great folds of their voluminous draperies glowing with colour among the warm shadows; on the other, at a reverend distance, enhanced by the verticals of the plain brick piers behind, the royal train mundane and restless with variety of colour; the grooms at the end standing carelessly by their horses in the full blaze of evening light.... This is is a tiny picture, youthful and naïve in much of its expression.
But in one figure at least there is a full taste of the visual poetry which was to make Venice famous in the sixteenth century.
(P. Hendy, *The National Gallery, London* 1960)

The use of canvas as a support had other consequences which regarded the execution of the painting and its effects more closely. The early canvases, made from extremely fine and closely-woven cloth, required a ground of smooth gesso, which was similar to that of a wood panel, therefore there was no significant change in the technique of painting. However, in the monochrome chiaroscuro by Mantegna it is possible to detect the weave of the canvas. It is difficult, though, to avoid seeing a relationship between the transformation of the technique of painting which took place in Venice around 1500 and the practice of painting on canvas. The new method of painting was a consequence of both the use of oil as a medium and canvas as a support—which allowed the use of direct brushwork without preliminary drawing—and, according to tradition, it was experimented for the first time by Giorgione. It was in this new manner, and in the cast of mind which it assumed, that the era of modern painting can be said to have begun.
(A. Chastel, *La grande officina*, 1966)

Giorgione was perhaps the first secular painter in the history of Italian art. His secularity was at the same time both formal and substantial. In the formal sense, in his work there was a kind of renunciation of religious narration, and this often led to the choice of another sphere of interest, unrelated to religious themes. This was not a polemical stand, but rather the beginning of an alternative kind of painting. It was possible to paint Madonnas—his works seemed to say—but it was also possible to paint people and landscapes, and even Madonnas as if they were people and landscapes. In this sense the end of painting as an expression of faith (inconceivable outside the context of the religious vision, even when the subject appeared quite worldly, while it was itself part and parcel of the sacred myth) began with Giorgione.
(V. Lilli, "Mito e laicismo di Giorgione," in *L'opera completa di Giorgione*, edited by P. Zampetti, 1968)

The myth of Giorgione developed parallel with the phenomenon of collecting by private individuals, first as the rush to buy up the artist's rare paintings just after his death..., then as a name—it did not matter whether it was true or false—which guaranteed a high market value for the work. From this point of view the myth of Giorgione is still quite solid today. Hence the demytholigisation of Giorgione must necessarily take place through a horizontal re-examination of the tendencies which lie behind the extremely complex art scene in Venice in the early sixteenth century.
From this re-examination it appears that the market, as far as the highest levels of patronage and the economic and cultural spheres were concerned, was saturated ... It was thanks to this saturation that an artist of Sebastiano's stature was forced to leave Venice, the disquieting ideas of Lorenzo Lotto were rejected in the provinces and Giorgione's role was socially circumscribed, while at the same time, without affecting its validity, fairly precise limits to the possibility

of his art being influential were established.
(A. Gentili, "Per la demitizzazione di Giorgione: documenti, ipotesi, provocazioni," in *Giorgione e la cultura veneta tra '400 e '500*, acts of the conference, 1978)

Thus by combining the two key moments of the history of Salvation, [in the *Three Philosophers*] Giorgione portrayed the Magi... In Giorgione's painting only the intense moment of expectation when the first faint light of the Star showed itself to humankind is depicted. This was the instant (of revelation or of discovery?) when human beings first came into contact with the new presence of God in the world. In the medieval iconographic tradition the Star *appears* to the Magi, almost compelling them to follow its glittering light. Sometimes an angel, the voice of God or the image of the infant Christ are added to the Star to lead them. In Giorgione's painting, on the contrary, it is the Magi who are *seeking* the Star, and they discover it as soon as it rises, staring intently into the gloomy depths of the cave. The apparition is immediately interpreted, not because an angel or the voice of God descends providentially from the heavens, but by careful inquiry, reading and taking measurements using astrologers' books, squares and compasses. And the divinity of the newborn child is not stressed by genealogy or an Annunciation, but it is *discovered* by men thanks to their science. The Star heralds a new era, which reveals that Christ is on earth, but it is human science which discovers this and makes it evident to all. By extracting this scene from the story of the Magi, Giorgione showed man exploring the world with his instruments and discovering the presence of God there, thus giving sacred history a temporal and human dimension.
(S. Settis, *La "Tempesta" interpretata. Giorgione, i committenti, il soggetto*, 1978)

It was Giorgione who interpreted, in the eyes of his contemporaries, the role of initiator of modern painting in Venice. This was despite (or, to a certain extent, because of) the relative lack of his paintings for public bodies... In the case of Giorgione, therefore, his most advanced experimentalism took place in the small paintings which the artist executed for his private patrons. Indeed, the revolution in painting was diffused by unexpected means. This is even more noticeable when extraordinary visual appeal is accompanied by themes which become progressively more obscure, resulting in paintings which have a large number of mysterious meanings... This also produced a strange contrast with the solemn, sometimes sublime, rearguard who were represented by the "public" painting. This does not refer so much to the large canvases which were being executed for the Doge's Palace—unknown to us because they were burnt in the 1577 fire—but rather the altarpieces or the narrative paintings for the *scuole*, in which there was no change from the work produced in the 1490s.
(M. Lucco, "La pittura a Venezia nel primo Cinquecento," in *La pittura in Italia. Il Cinquecento*, 1988)

Having recently finished his apprenticeship, Titian then first became known through the Fondaco frescoes. But not even in this work was it possible to distinguish many signs of dependence on supposed masters. On the contrary, his work appears to have been unrelated even to that of Giorgione, who, although he worked only a few metres away, resembled Titian only to the most inexpert Venetians, who confused his work with that of the young artist from Cadore and paid him compliments which to Giorgione sounded like the worst kind of affront. If, in fact, we observe the *Justice*, which was the cause of scandal due to the very unfortunate faux pas, and we compare it with Giorgione's *Nude*, the very different spirit which inspired the younger artist vis-à-vis that of the colleague, who was by then well-established, is evident. The figure in Titian's fresco is dynamic and vigorous in her pose as she brandishes a sword and tramples a bloody head underfoot, whereas Giorgione withdraws into stylish elegance. It is sharply drawn and realistic in the colour, which tends to create a sensual effect even though only a shoulder is bared, while Giorgione, even though he presents total nudity, seems to take refuge in artificial chromatic abstraction.
(T. Pignatti, *Giorgione e Tiziano*, catalogue of the exhibition, Palazzo Ducale, Venice 1990)

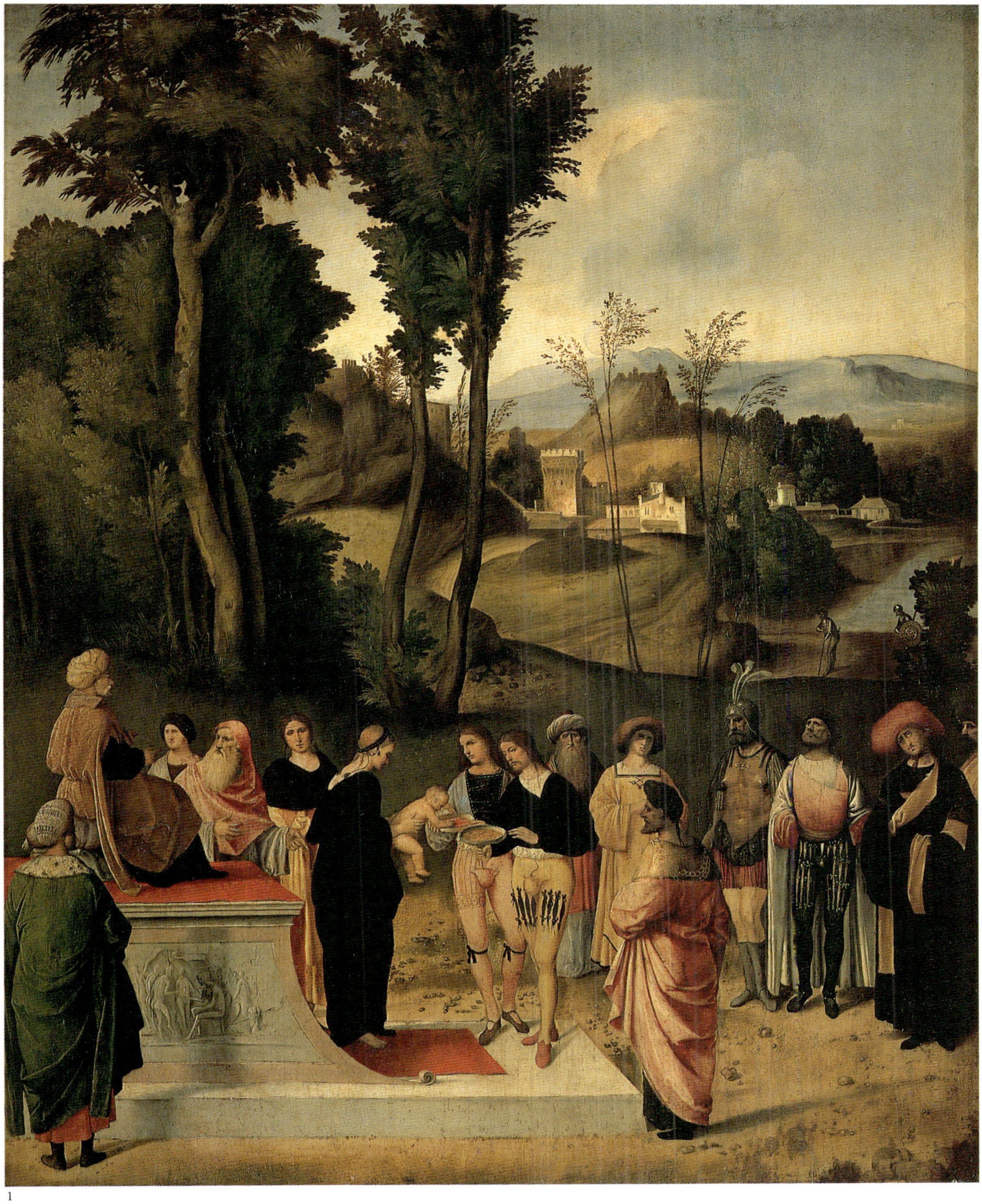

1

1-3. The Trial of Moses; The Judgement of Solomon, *1500-1505, panels, 89 x 72 cm each. Galleria degli Uffizi, Florence. The two paintings, which are evidently closely linked to each other, are among the first known works by Giorgione. The details of the landscape and the figures are still sharply defined, with the strong light giving them precise outlines. The doubts concerning attribution are justified by stylistic inconsistency, above all in the depiction of the figures. As often happened in his short career, Giorgione collaborated with another artist, perhaps of Ferrarese origin.*

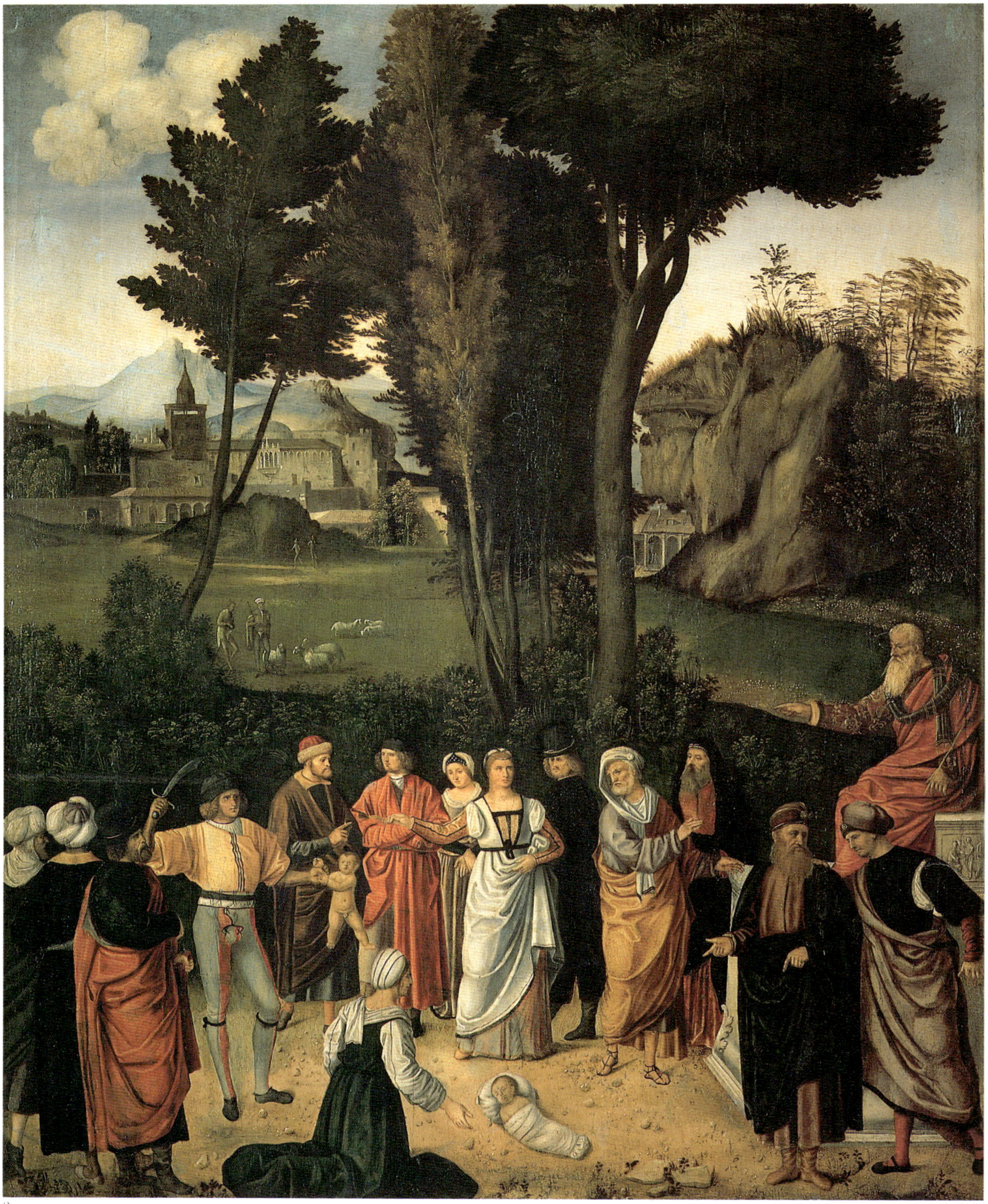

2

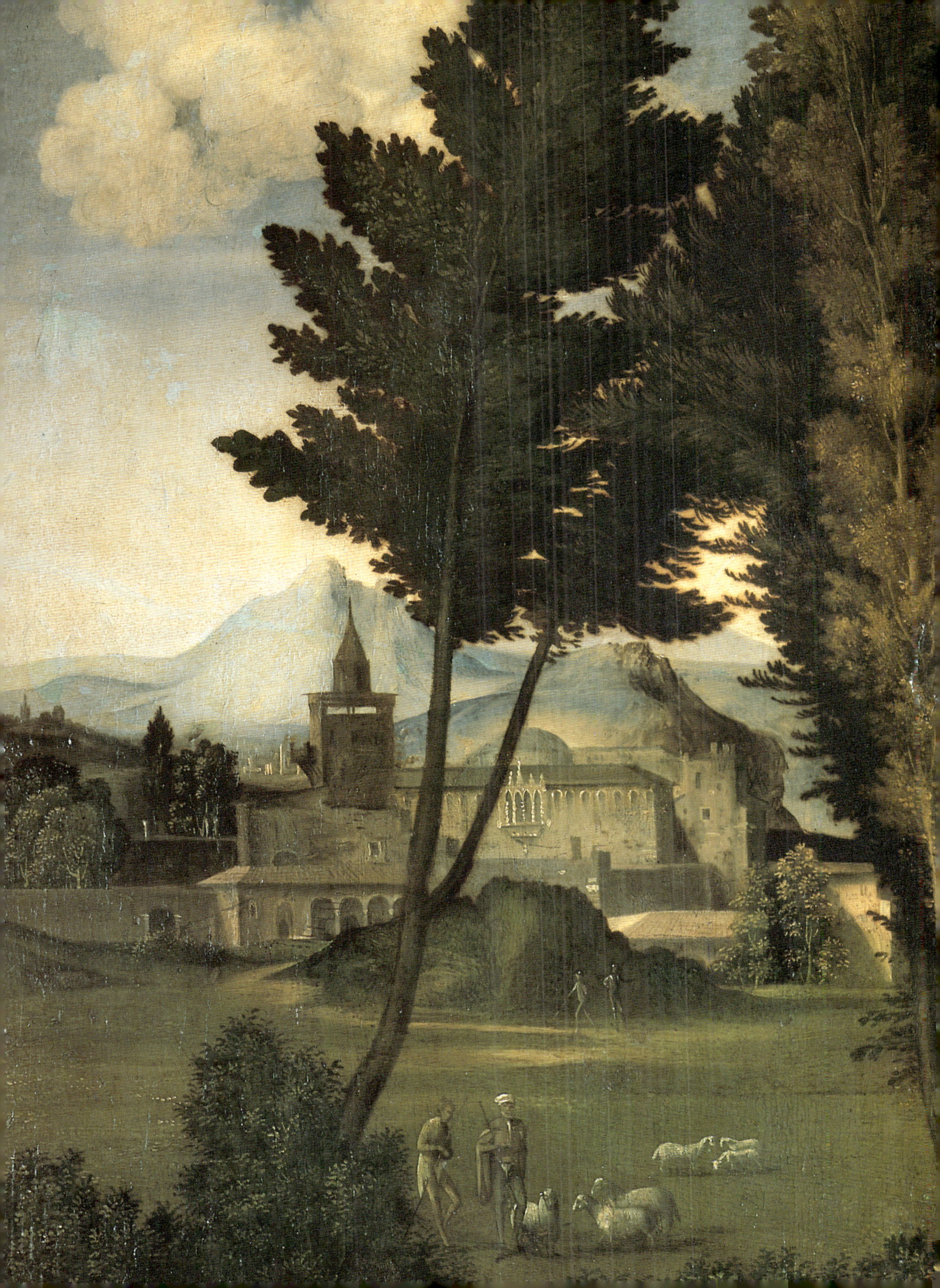

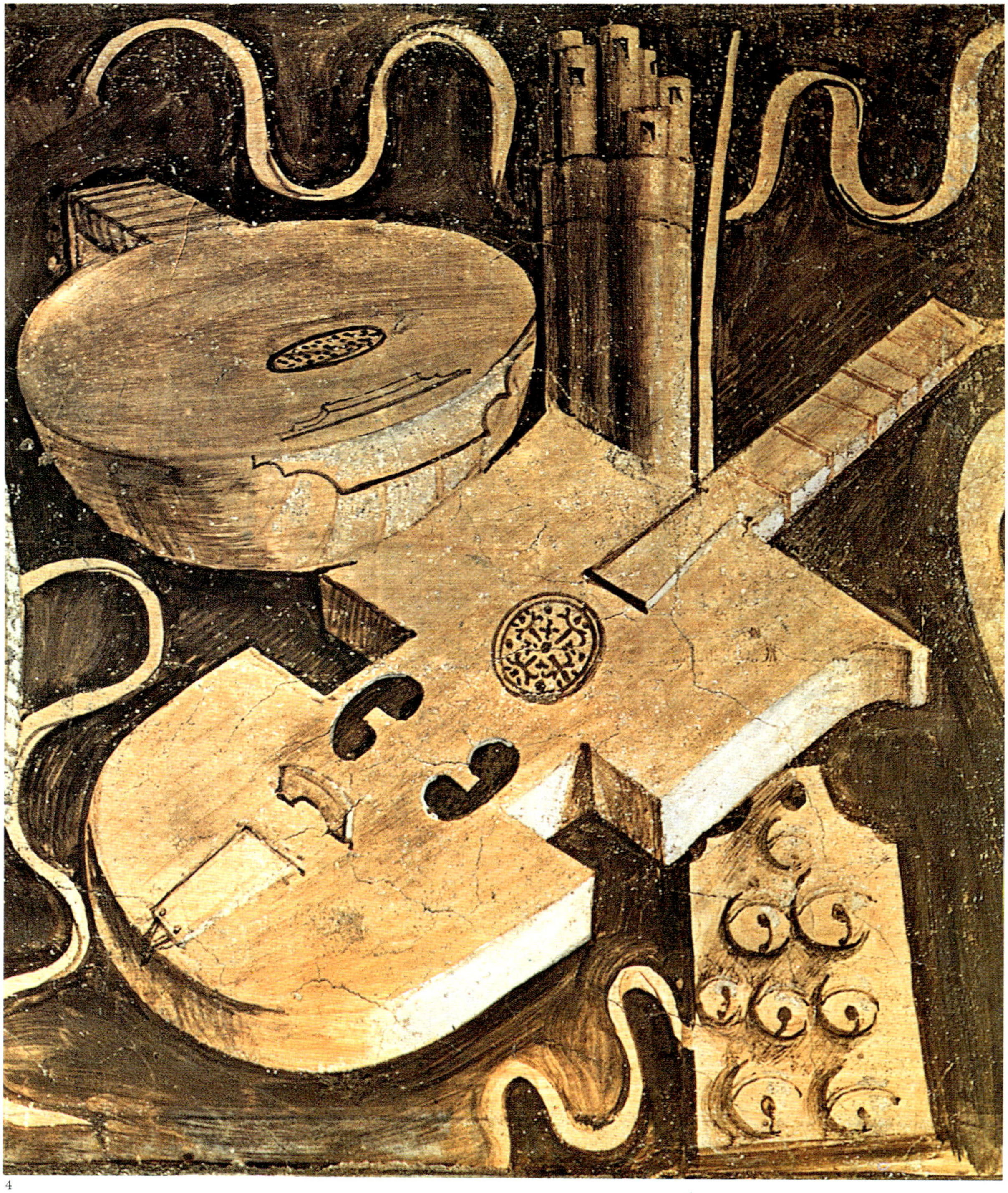

4

4. Frieze with Instruments of the Liberal Arts, *1500-1505, fresco. Casa Pellizzari (or "Casa del Giorgione"), Castelfranco Veneto. It is a long monochrome frieze, only partly preserved, which decorates a room in the so-called "Casa del Giorgione" in Castelfranco. Making use of perspective, a sequence of objects and research instruments alternates with inscriptions and portraits of thinkers.*

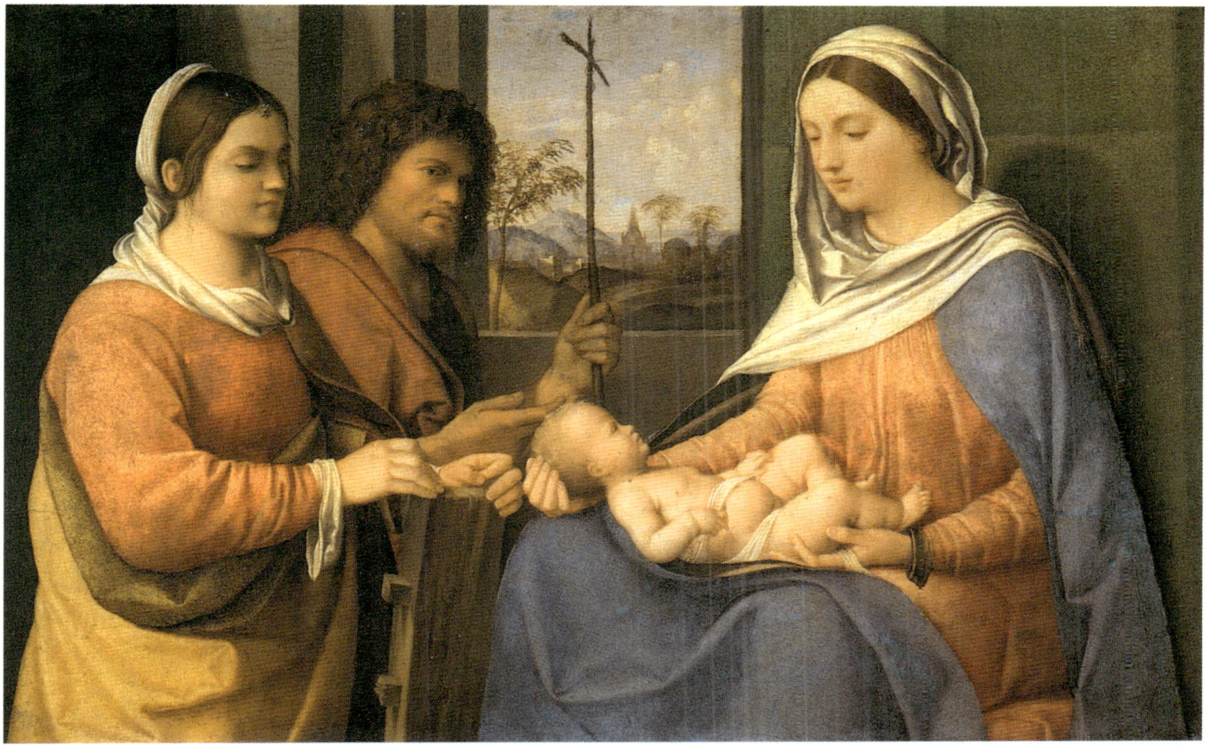

5

5. Giorgione and Sebastiano del Piombo, Madonna with Saint Catherine and Saint John the Baptist, *c. 1505, panel, 51 x 81 cm. Gallerie dell'Accademia, Venice. This small painting, in a good state of conservation, was produced for private devotion. The calm disposition of the figures in a peacefully illuminated space corresponds to a typically Giorgionesque concept. Some scholars believe that this painting was executed with the help of the young Sebastiano del Piombo, who served his apprenticeship in close contact with Giorgione's circle, to the extent that he collaborated in the painting of the* Three Philosophers.

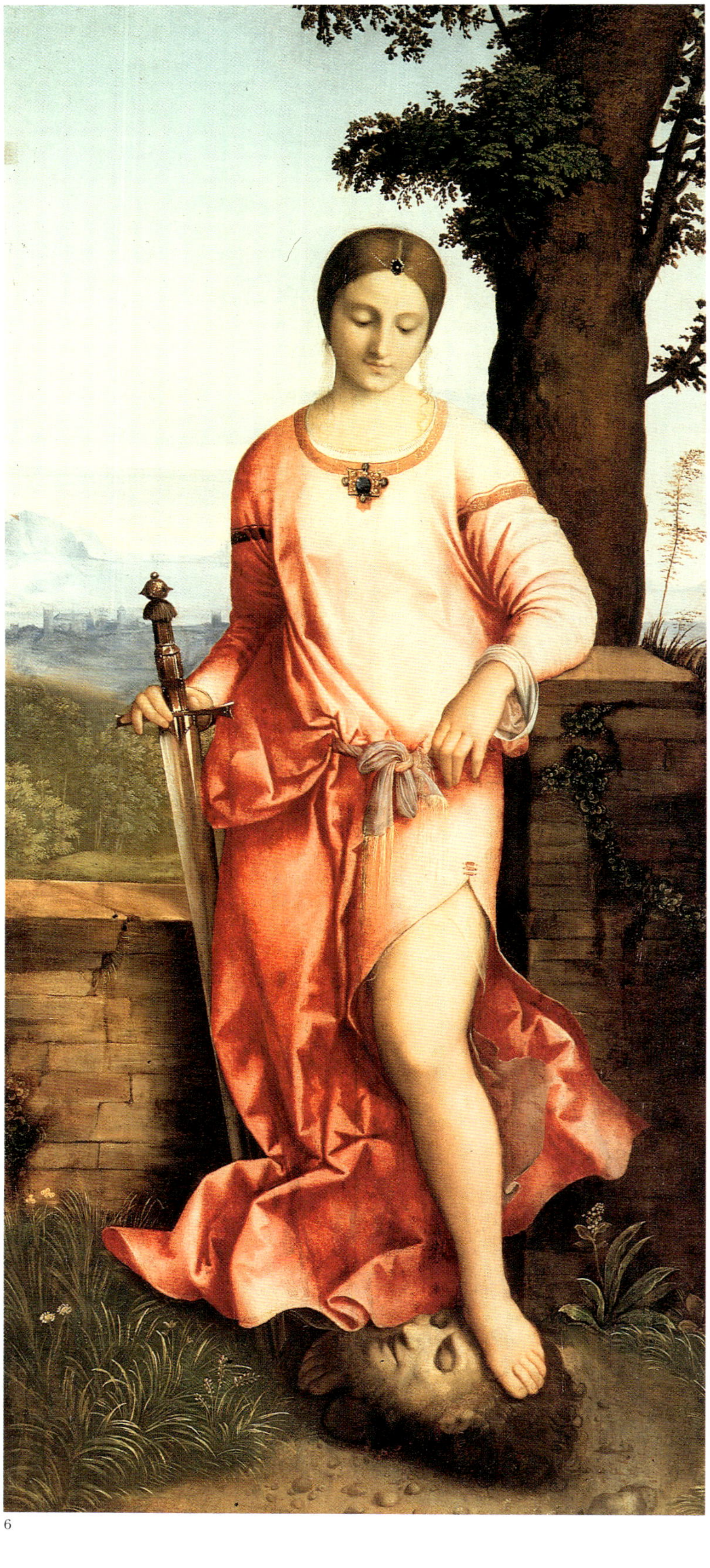

6

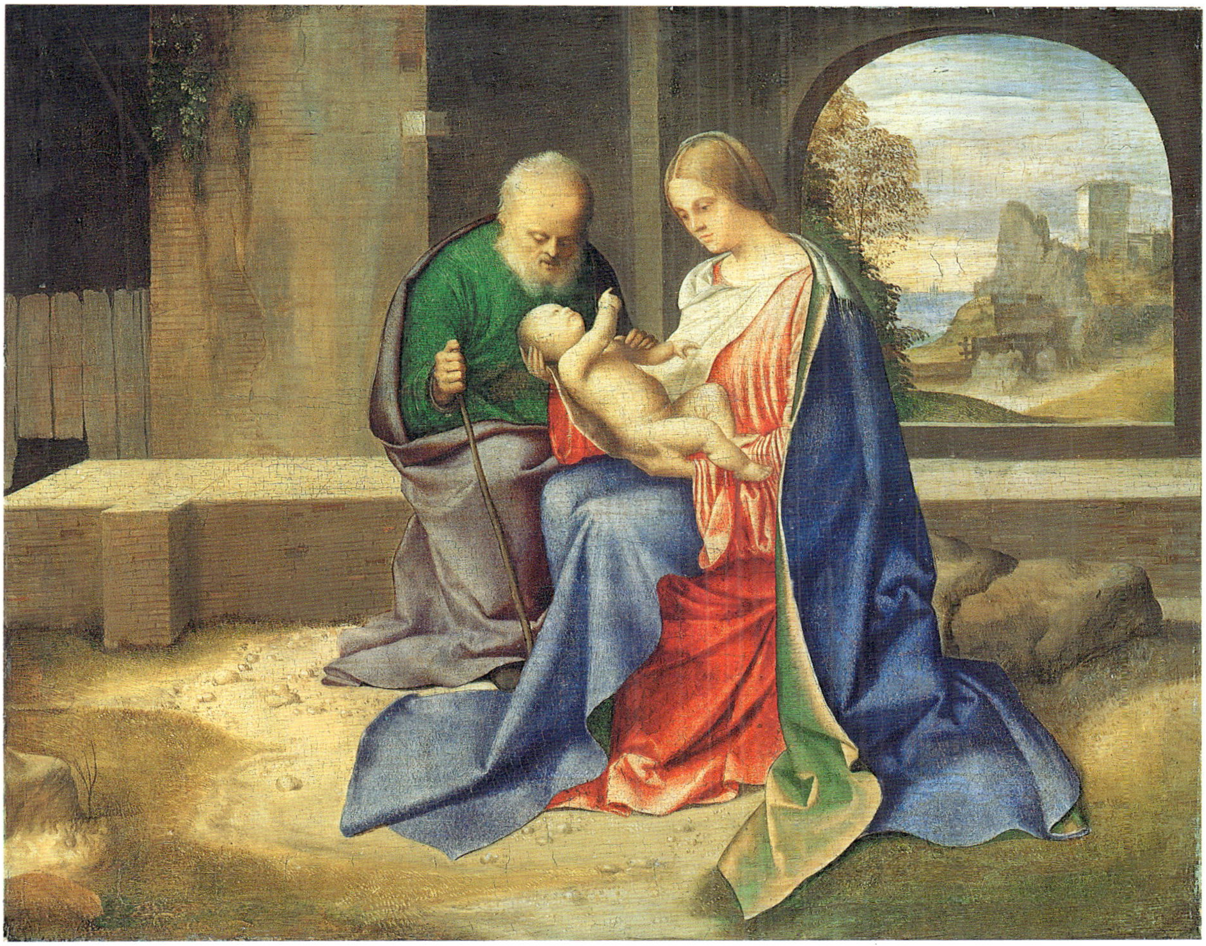

7

6. Judith. *c.1503, panel transferred to canvas, 144 x 66 cm. Hermitage, Leningrad.*
As can be seen from comparison with old engravings, the painting has been cut down on the sides. The sunset in the background allowed Giorgione to experiment with the effects of low light, which was an important stage in the conscious achievement of the technique of tonality.

7. Holy Family *(or* Benson Madonna*), c.1504, panel, 37x45 cm. National Gallery of Art, Washington.*
A number of analogies with Flemish art, in particular the folds of the Virgin's mantle, enhance this small painting, which is a typical product of private devotion. This type of composition assured the young Giorgione of success in the cultural circles of the Venetian aristocracy.

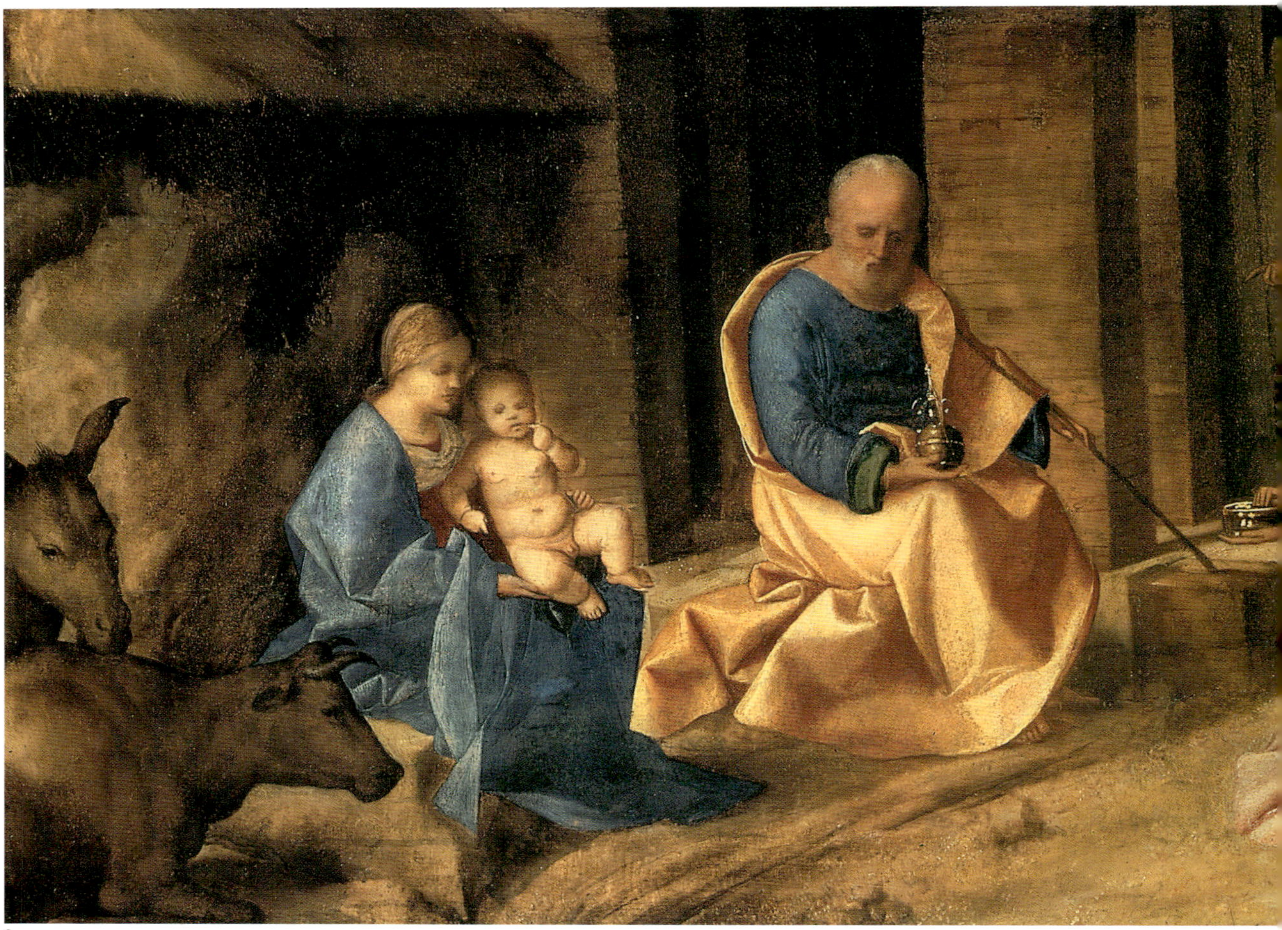

8

8. Adoration of the Magi, *c.1504, panel, 29 x 81 cm. National Gallery, London.*
The elongated shape of the painting suggested to Giorgione a clear division of the scene into two parts, which is stressed by the brick wall. The Holy Family on the left is seated in peaceful shadows, while the Magis' retinue, in which there are brightly dressed grooms, is completely in the light.

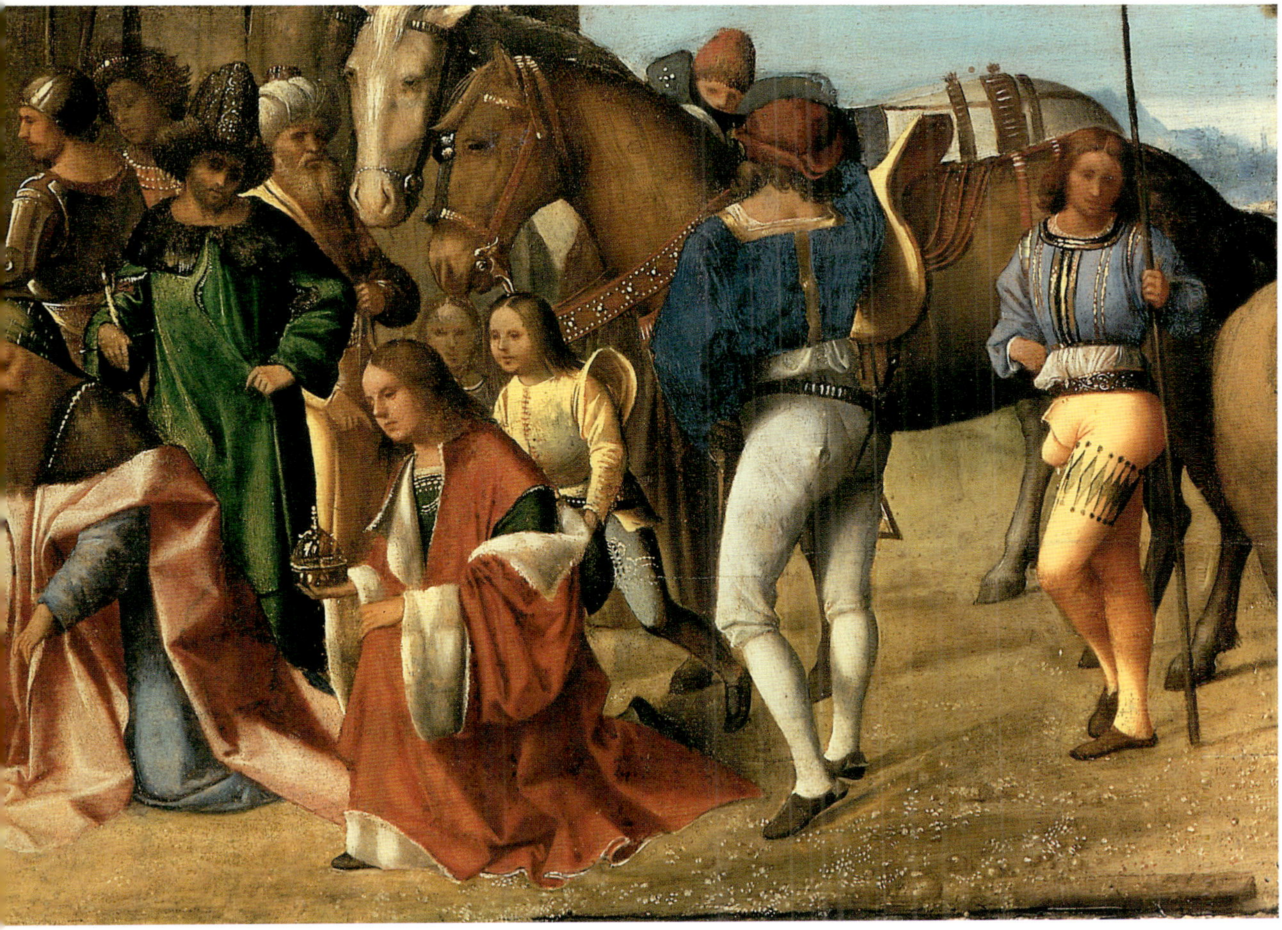

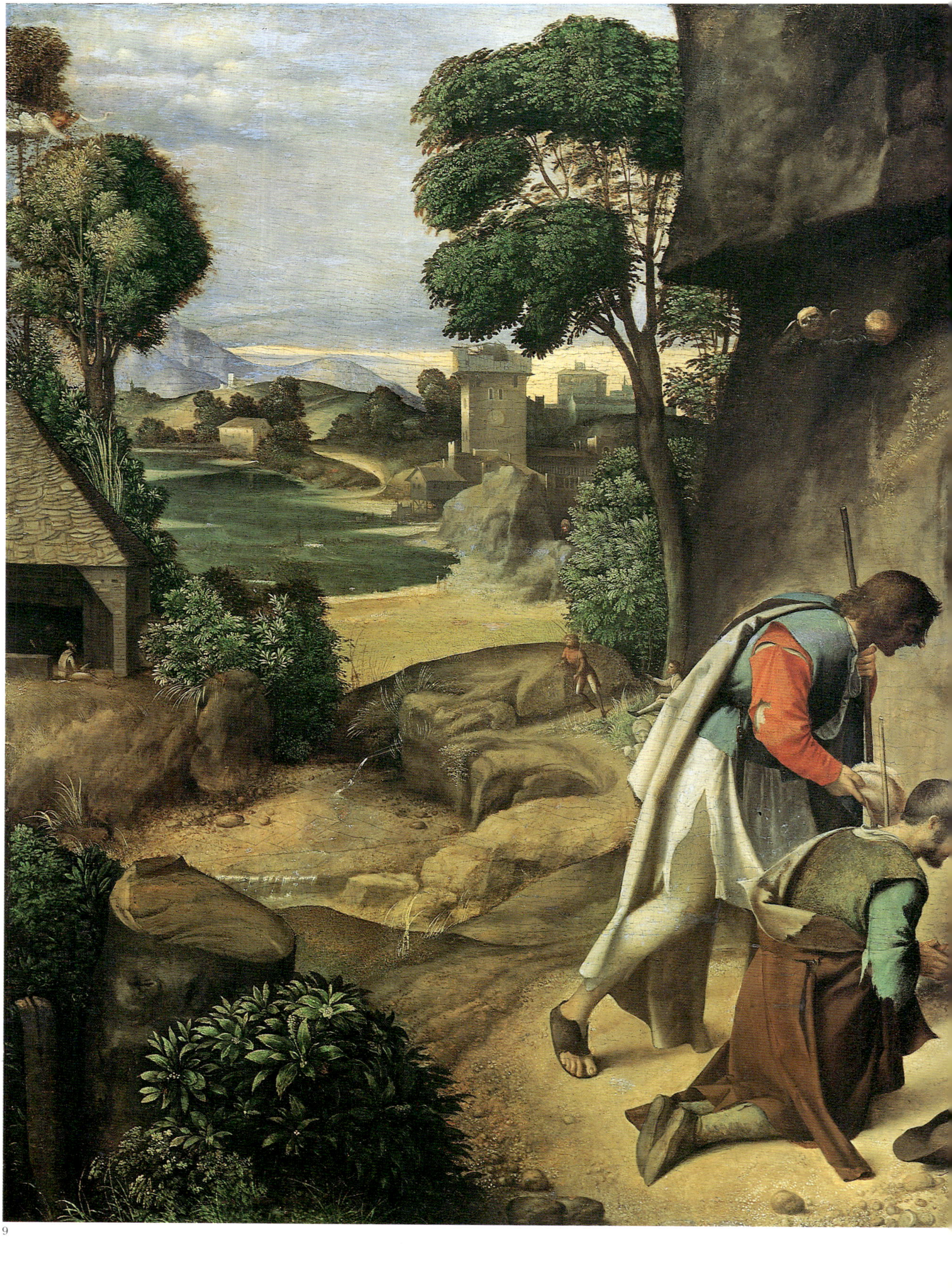

9

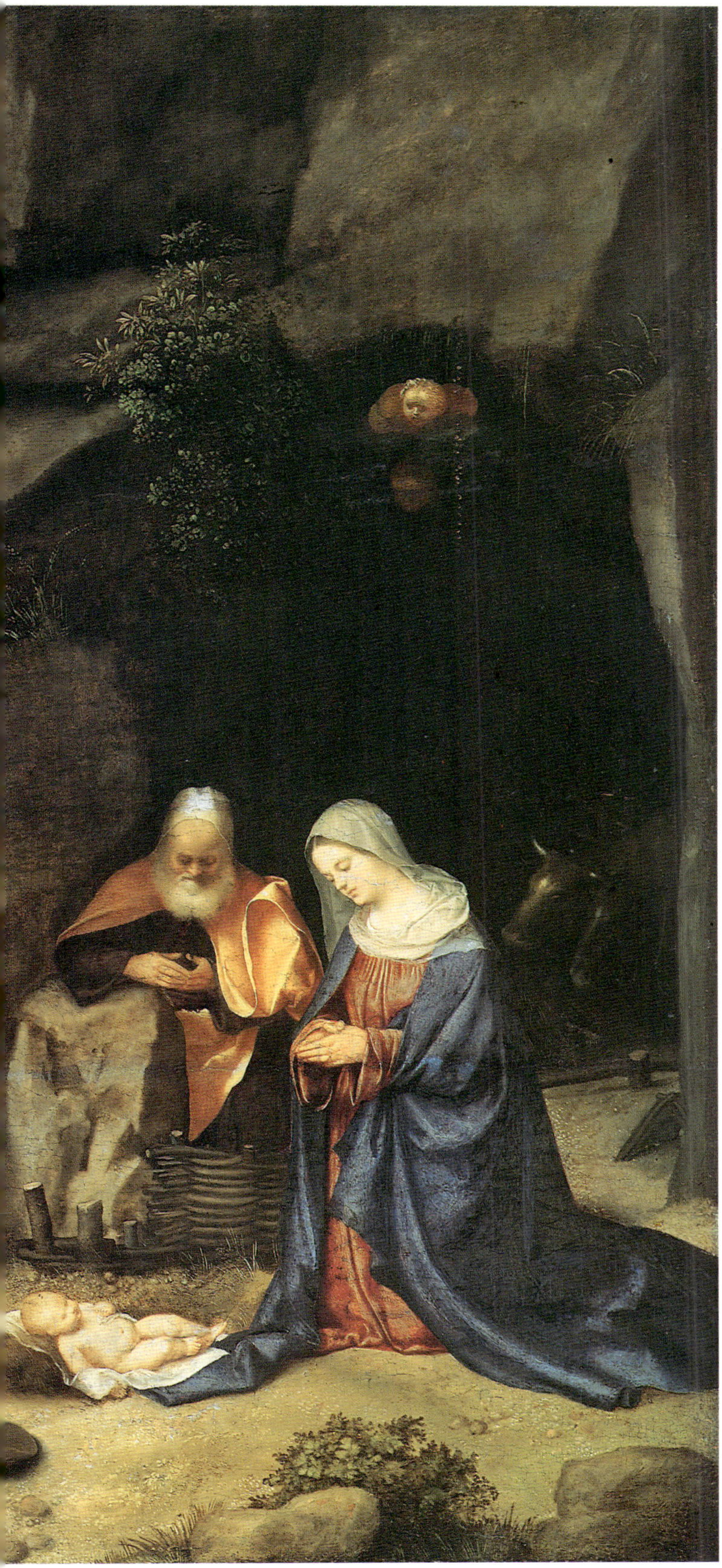

9. Adoration of the Shepherds *(or* Allendale Nativity*), c.1504, panel, 91 x 111 cm. National Gallery of Art, Washington.*
This painting marks the high point in the series of religious themes painted by Giorgione during his early years. A replica, with slight variations, exists in the Kunsthistorisches Museum in Vienna. The figures are concentrated in a corner of the painting in order to leave the maximum possible space to the landscape, which is no longer merely the background, but participates directly in the theme thanks to the subtle atmospheric definition of every detail.

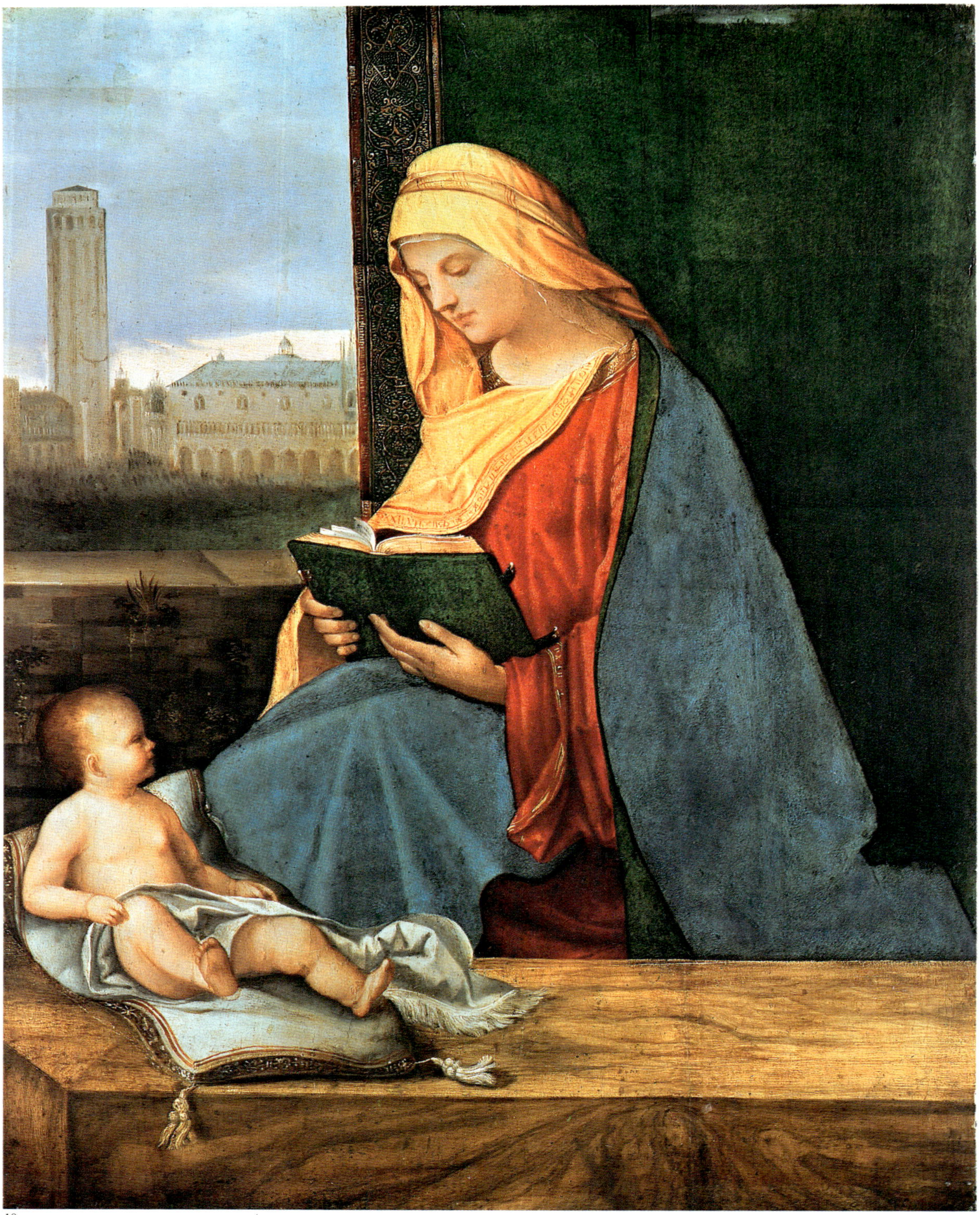

10

10, 11. Virgin and Child with a View of Venice Behind *(also known as the* Madonna Reading *or* Tallard Madonna*), c.1504, panel, 76 x 60 cm. Ashmolean Museum, Oxford. A rare example of a painting in an interior by Giorgione, who nearly always chose country settings for his religious compositions. In this case, the weak light increases the sense of concentration, while the window opens onto the veiled panorama of the Piazzetta di San Marco (perhaps unfinished).*

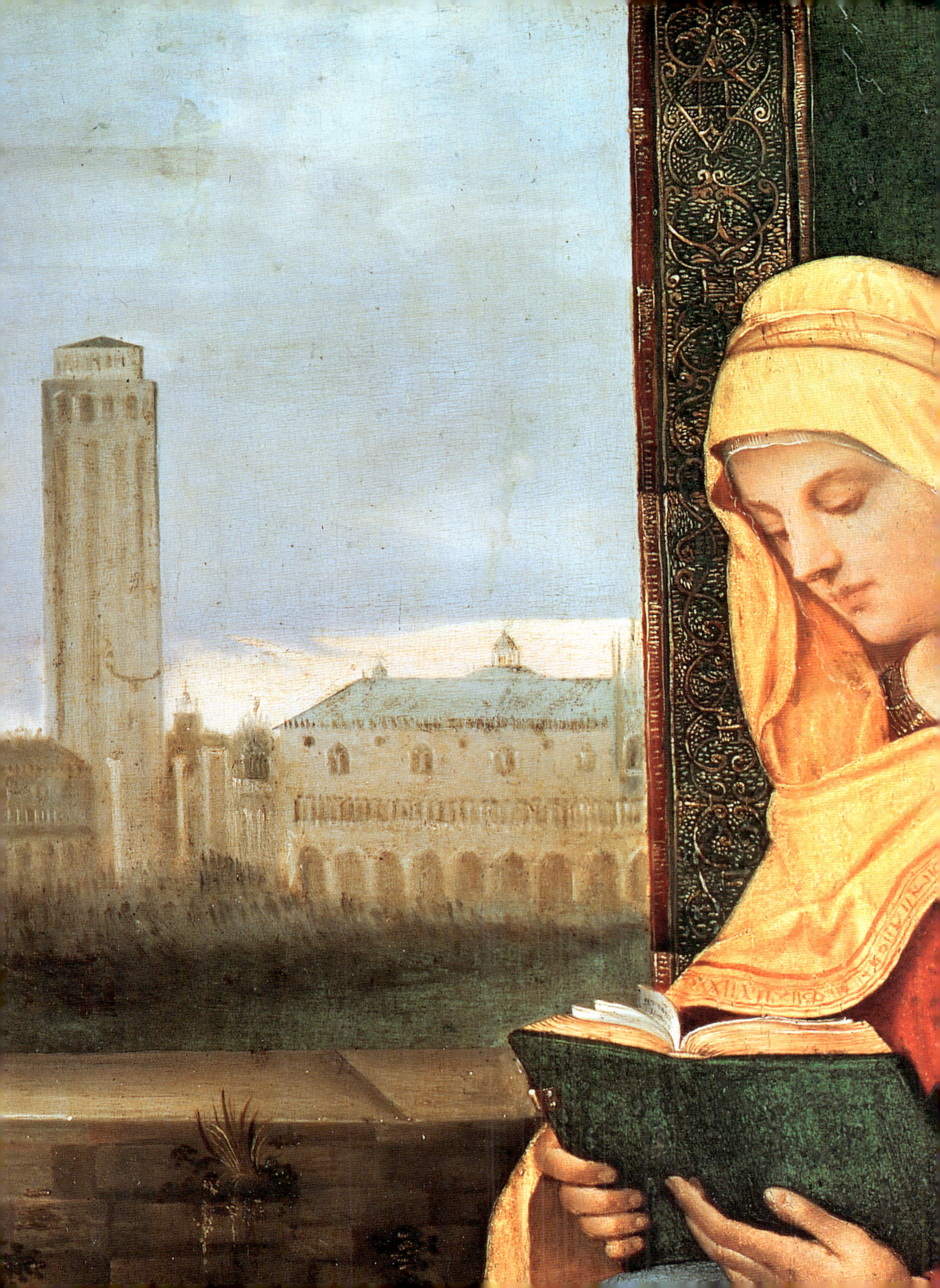

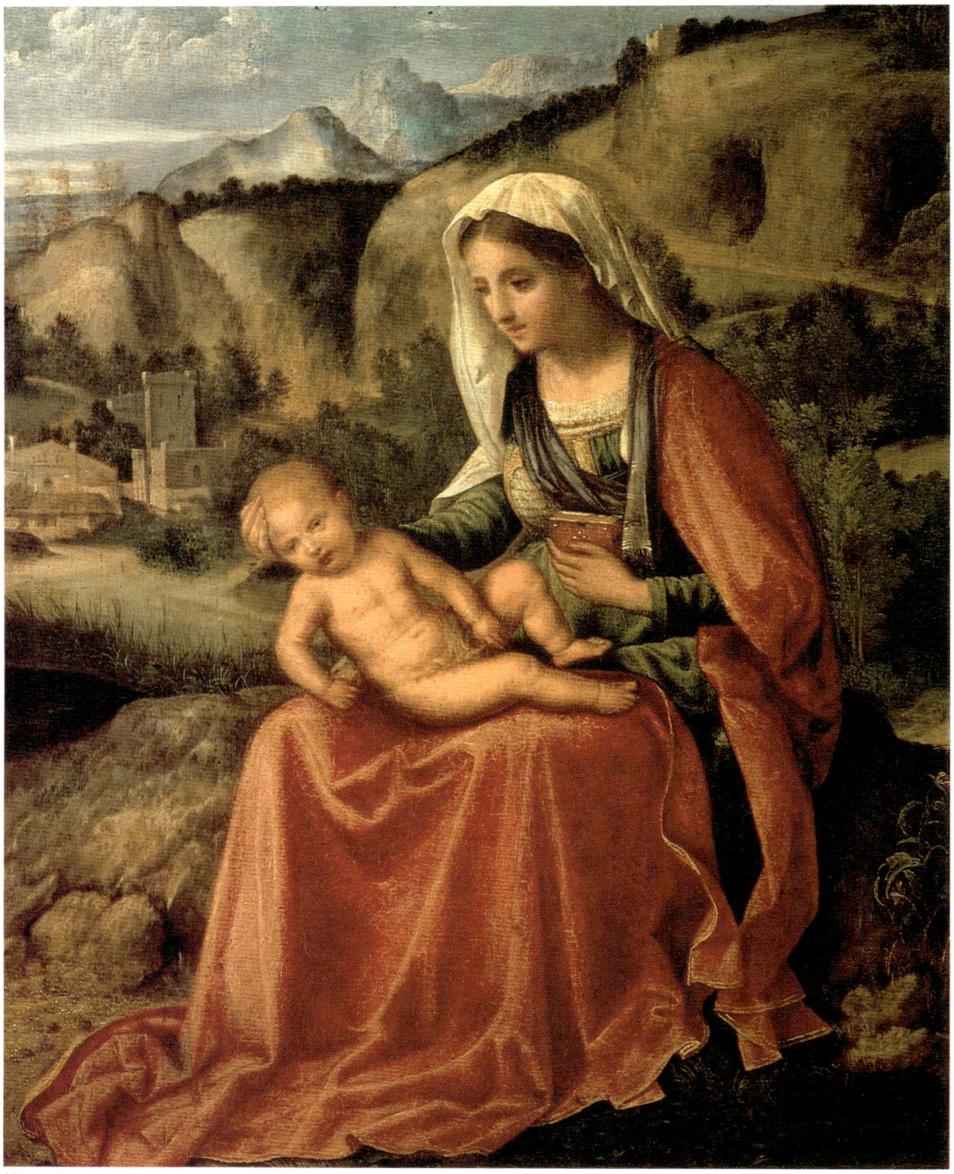

12

12. Madonna and Child, *c. 1505, canvas, 44 x 36 cm. Hermitage, Leningrad.*
The painting has been widely studied and has had various attributions; finally, in the sixties, it was attributed to Giorgione on the basis of clear analogies with works executed prior to the Castelfranco Altarpiece, *especially in the drapery, in which there is an echo of engravings by Martin Schongauer.*

13-15. Castelfranco Altarpiece (Enthroned Madonna with Saint Liberale and Saint Francis), *1504-1505, panel, 200 x 152 cm. Cathedral, Castelfranco Veneto.*
Commissioned by Tuzio Costanzo, it is the only certain work by Giorgione which was painted for a church.
The pyramidal structure, with the Madonna flanked symmetrically by two saints, follows the traditional model of the sacra conversazione.
However, Giorgione omitted many architectural features in order to leave space free for the landscape and, above all, the light, which is diffused uniformly in the whole painting.
The modestly sized altarpiece was a turning point in the establishment of tonality, in other words of painting based on the gradation of tones of light and colour on the image, limiting, or totally eliminating, the use of precisely drawn outlines.

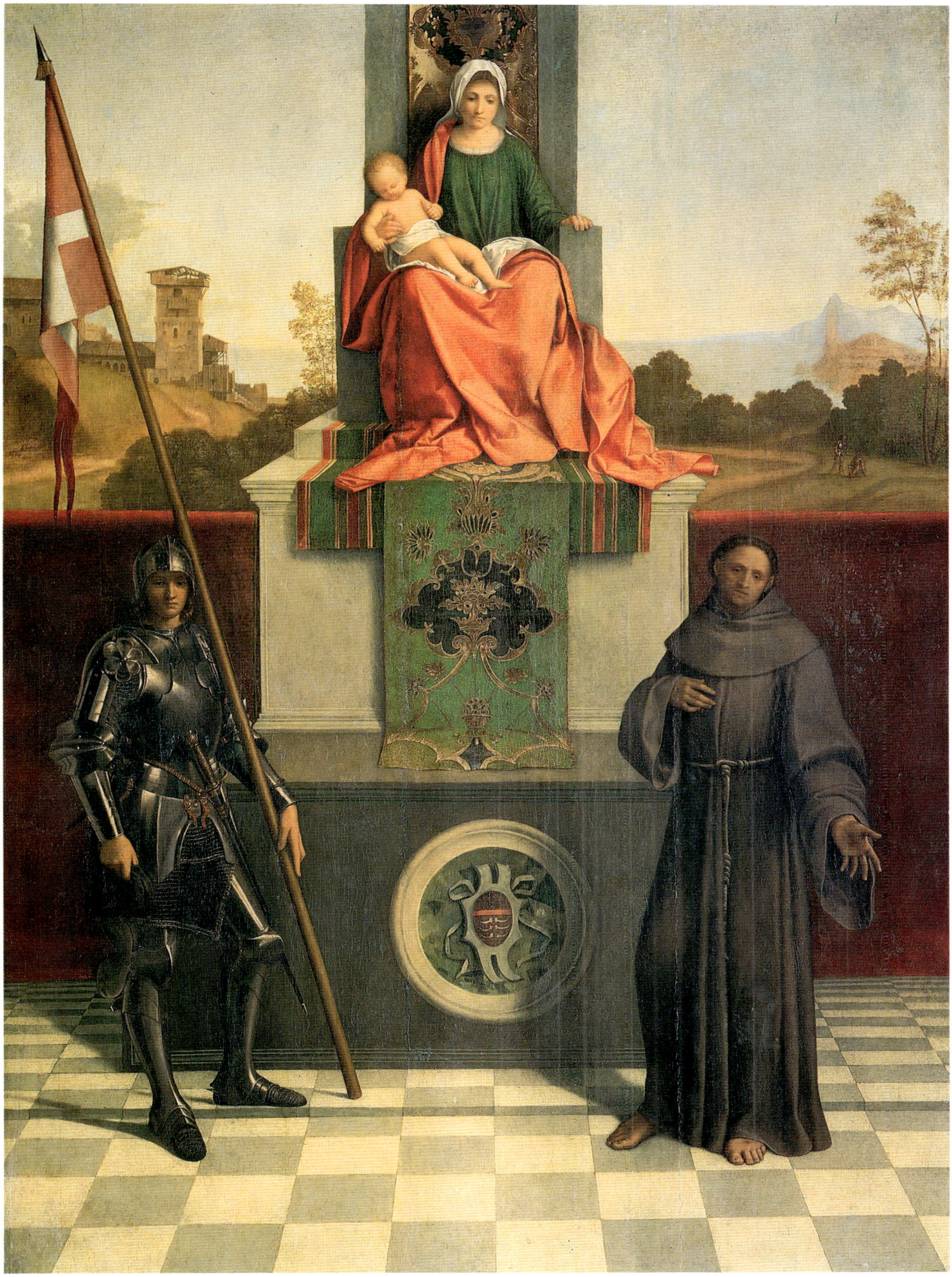

13

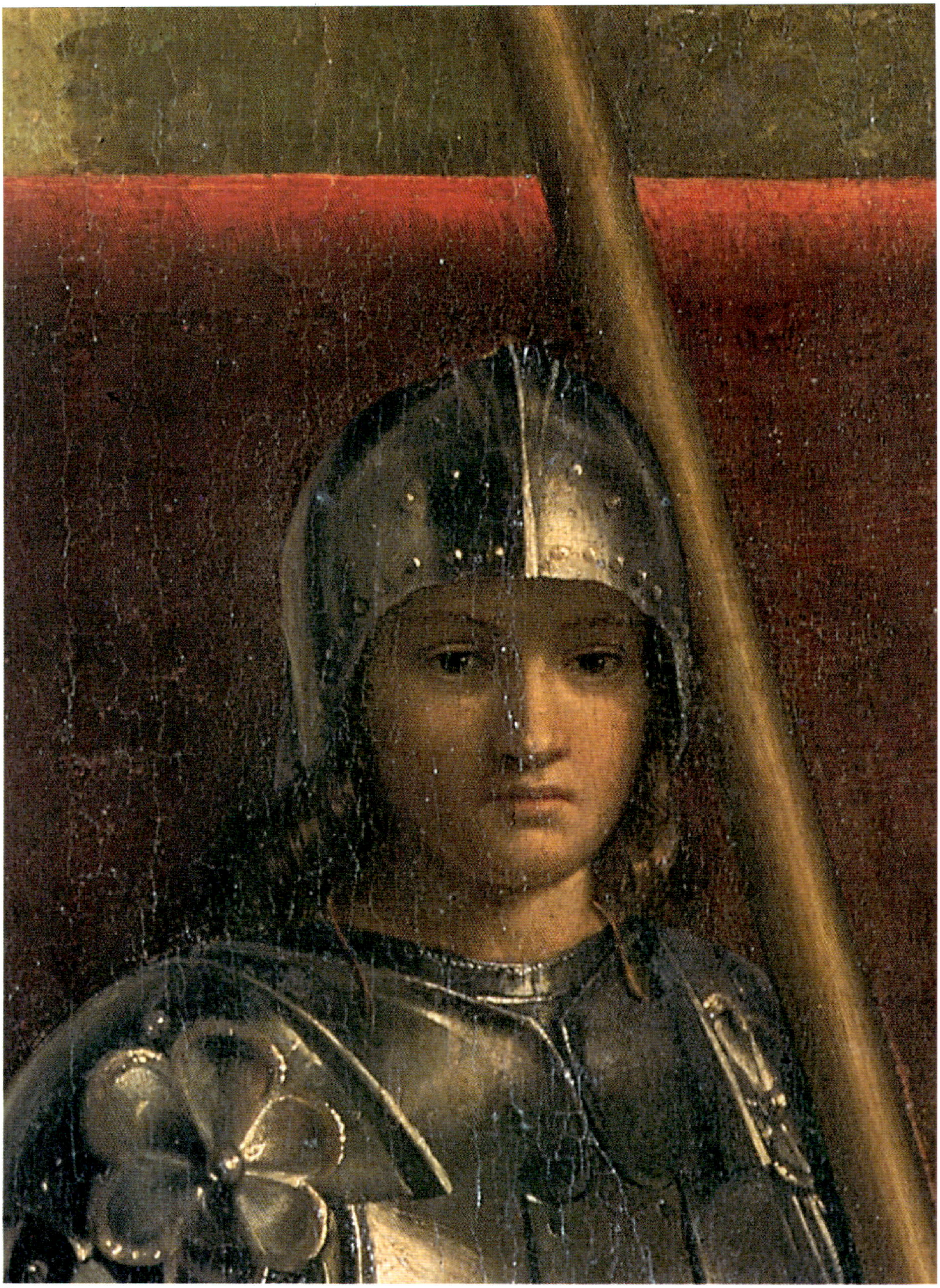

14

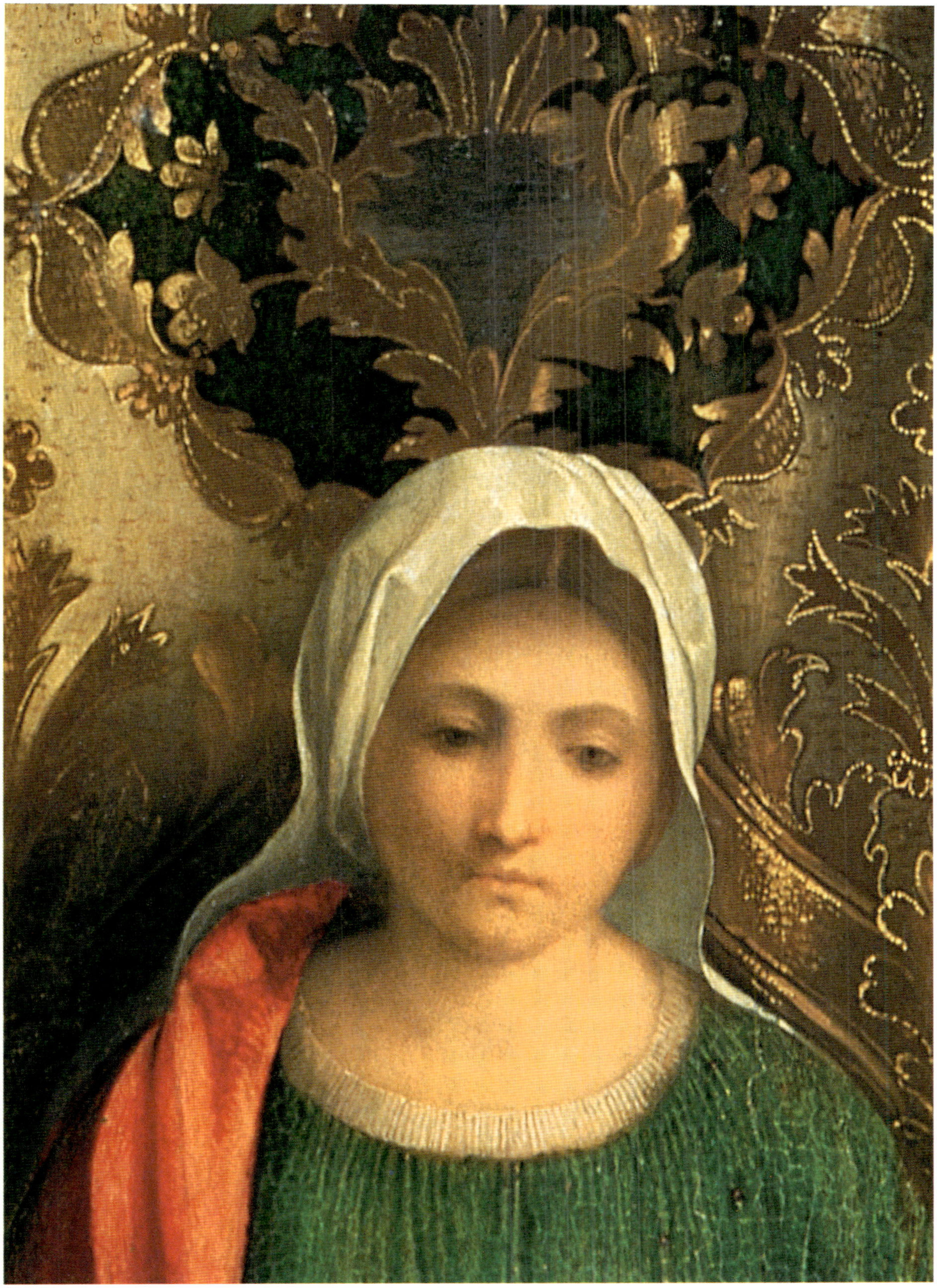

15

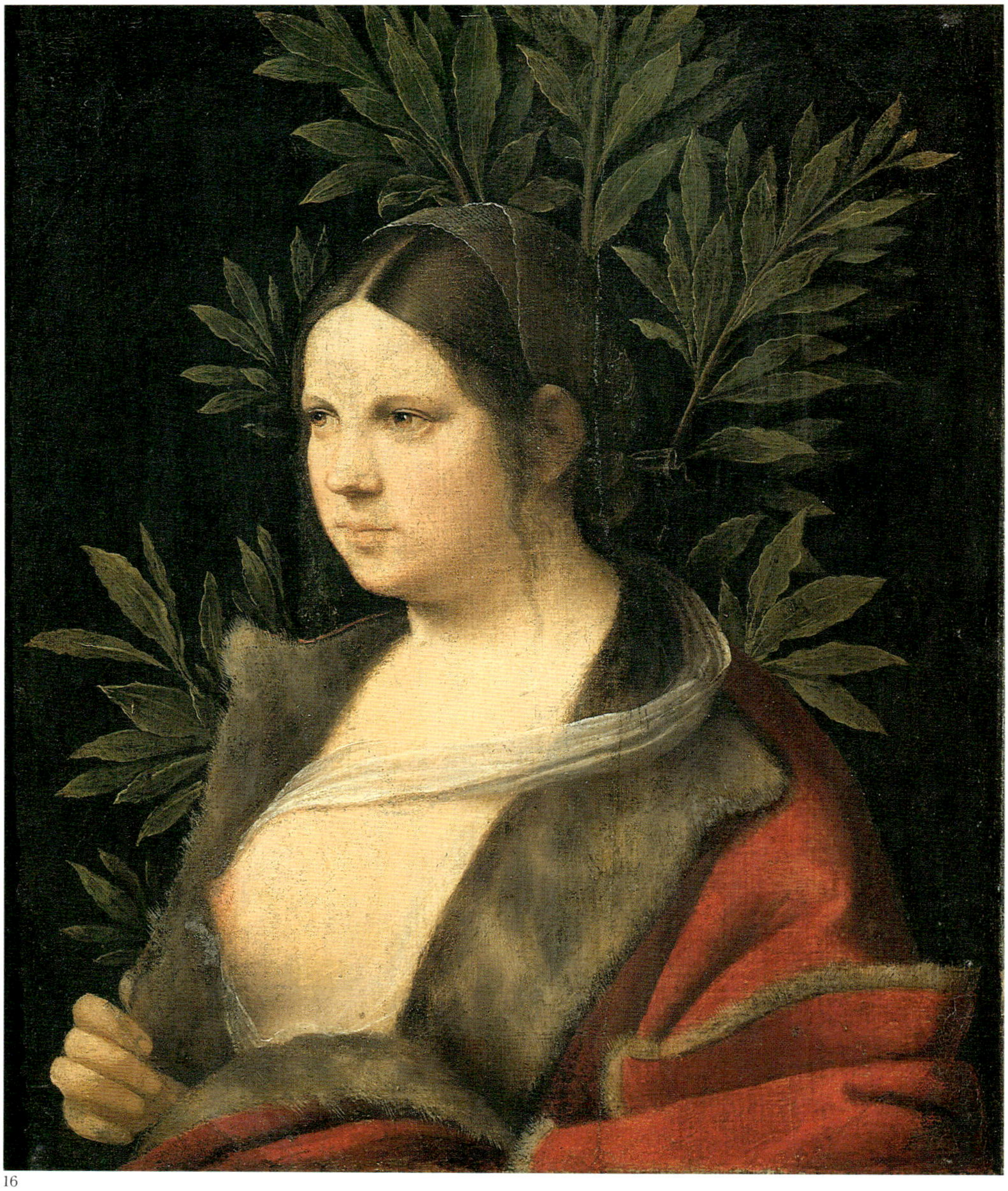

16

16. Laura*, 1506, canvas on panel, 41 x 33 cm. Kunsthistorisches Museum, Vienna.*
An inscription on the back allows us to date this painting with precision. The name of the girl (the same model who appeared in The Tempest*, Plates 17, 18) derives from the laurel leaves which appear behind her. According to contemporary sources, Giorgione started the fashion for this kind of painting featuring half-length portraits of young maidens in full bloom. In fact, the theme became very popular in the following ten years, and was also taken up by Titian.*

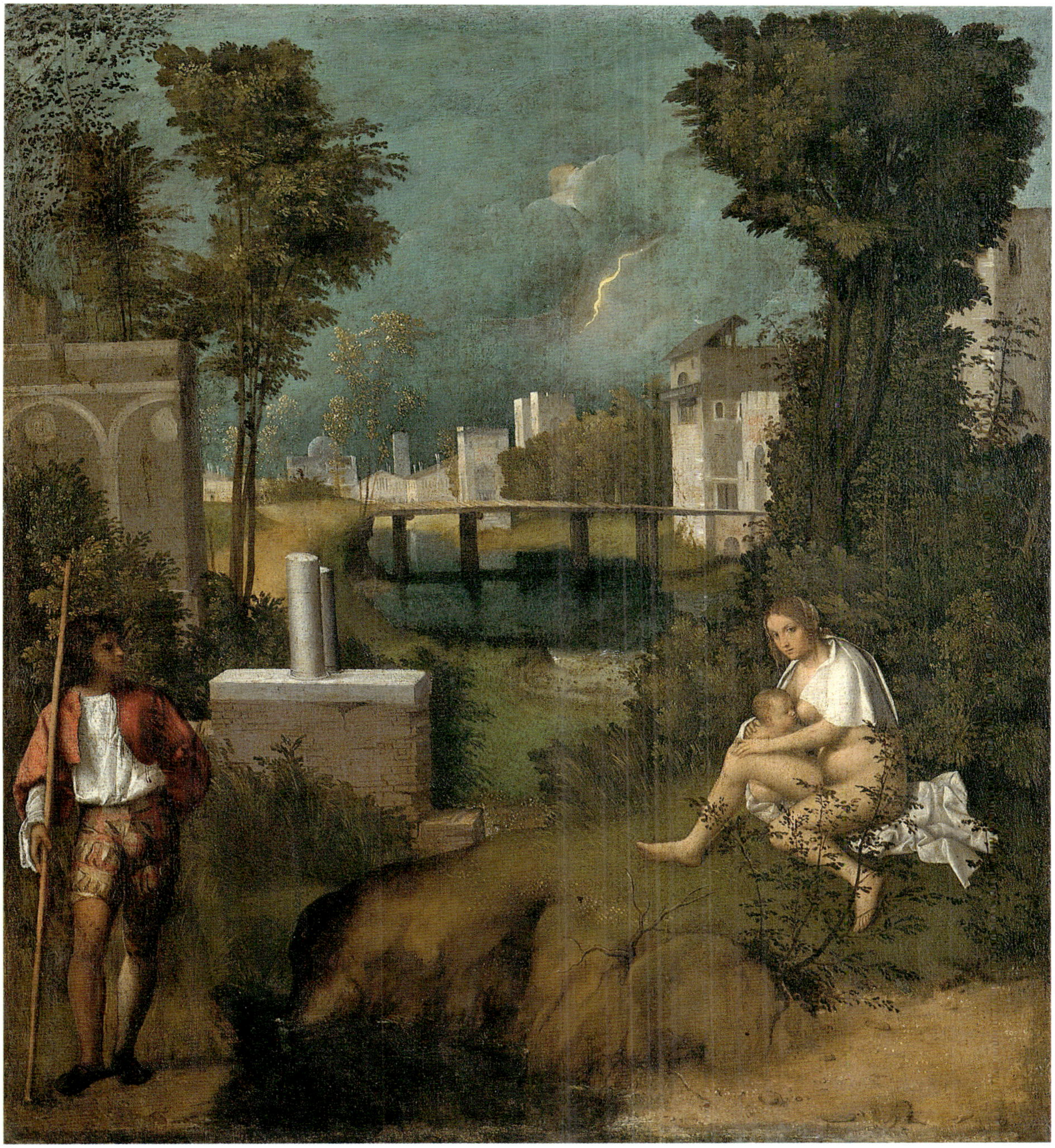

17

17, 18. The Tempest, *c. 1506, canvas, 82 x 73 cm. Gallerie dell'Accademia, Venice. Among the very few paintings by Giorgione which was documented by the sources, there has been a vast amount of research into its theme. The most recent theories consider that the two figures may represent Adam and Eve after their expulsion from Paradise, but apart from this it is really a painting about landscape. For the buildings and ruins in the background and the lush vegetation, Giorgione abandoned the precise definition of the early paintings and used a richer, mellower palette. The detail of the trees allows us to appreciate the patient, delicate texture of the light which gives the painting extraordinary and original appeal.*

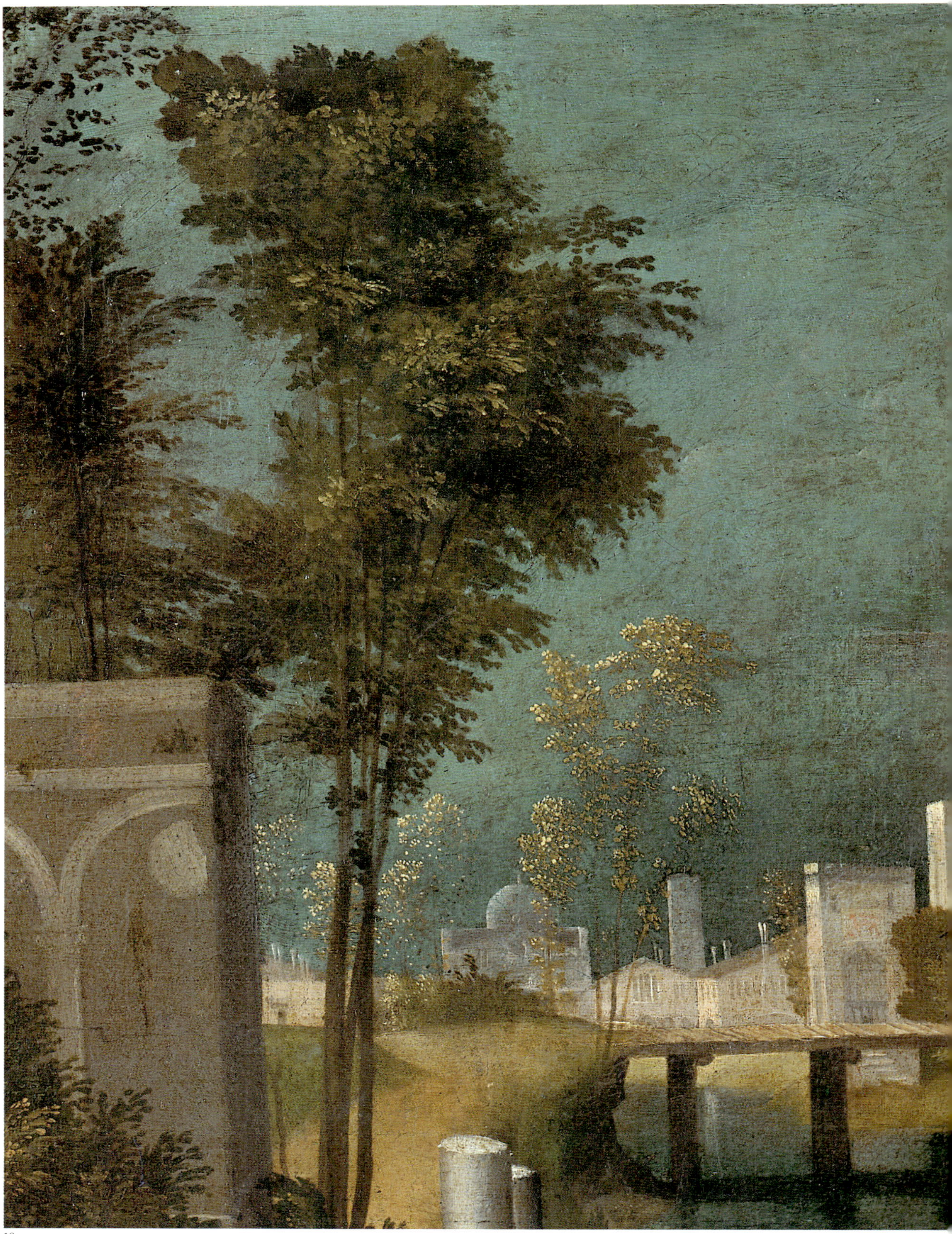

18

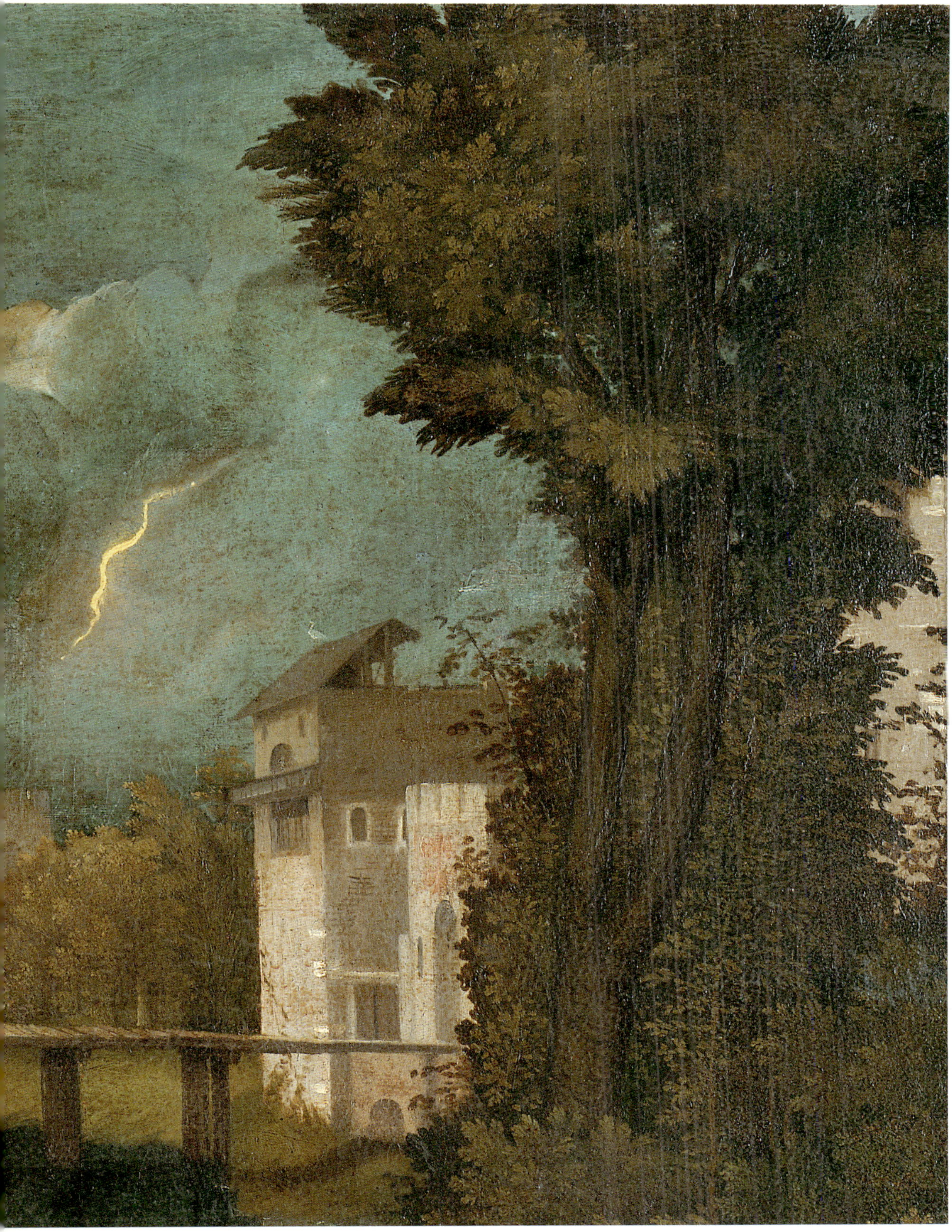

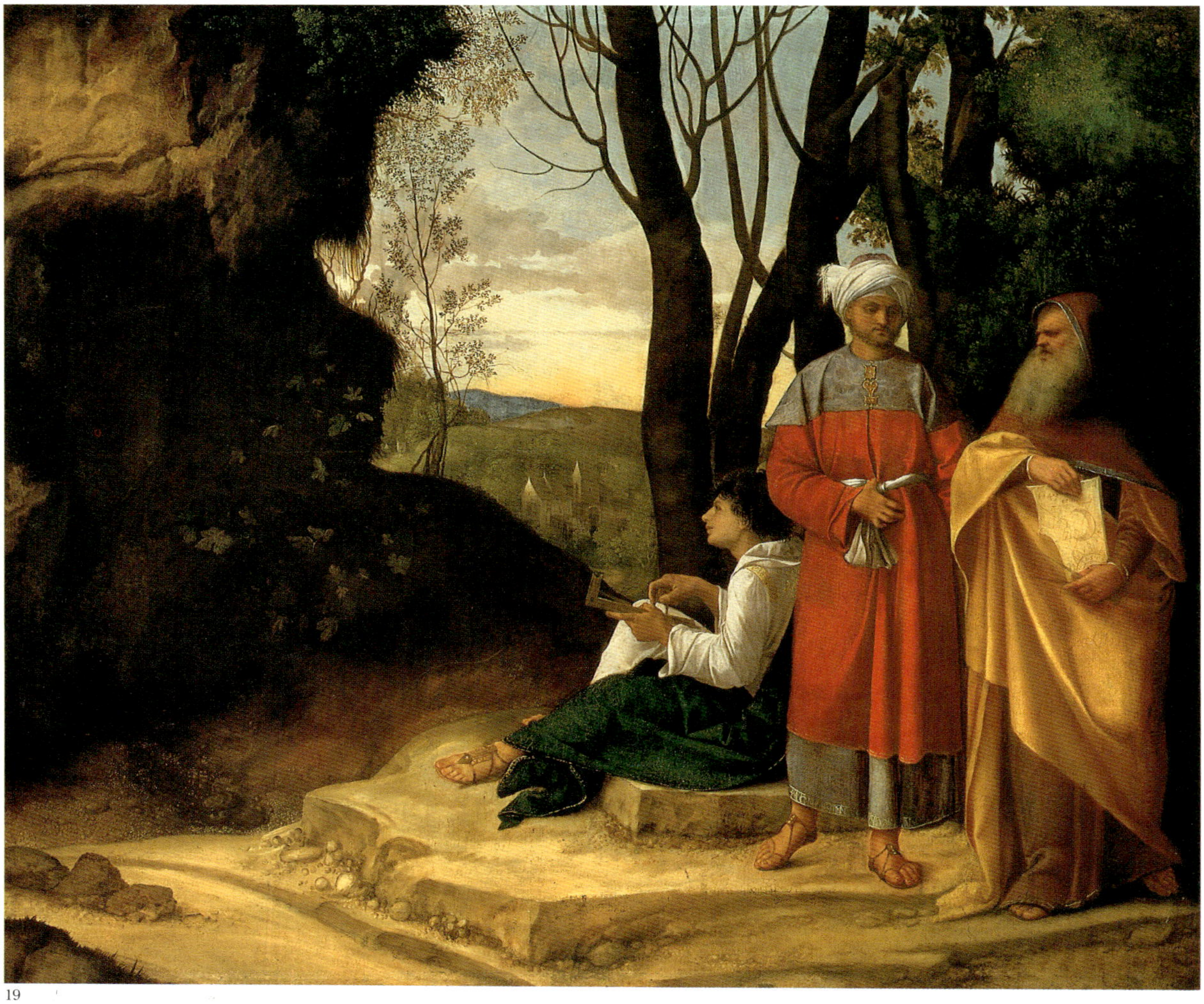

19

19, 20. Three Philosophers, *after 1505, canvas, 123 x 144 cm. Kunsthistorisches Museum, Vienna. The painting was executed at the midpoint of Giorgione's artistic career. The colours are extremely vivid, but they are skilfully blended within the atmospheric light. The sense of expectation and research, and the careful interpretation of a number of iconographic details have caused scholars to think that the "three philosophers" (sometimes simply interpreted as an allegory of the so-called "three ages of man," a theme which was extremely popular in the Venetian art world in the early sixteenth century) might be astronomers, or even the three Magi observing the first appearance of the star. According to old sources, the landscape was completed by Sebastiano del Piombo.*

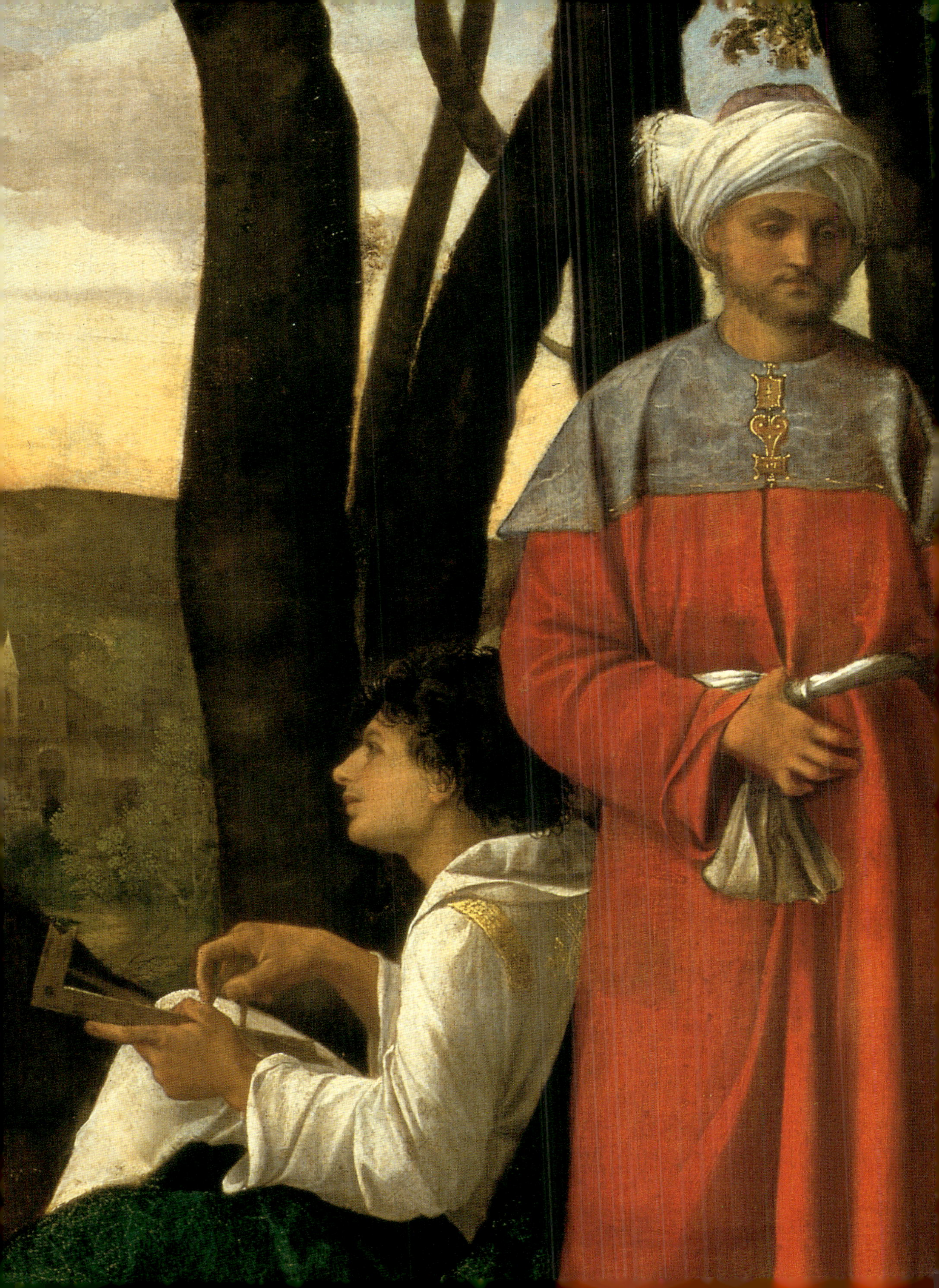

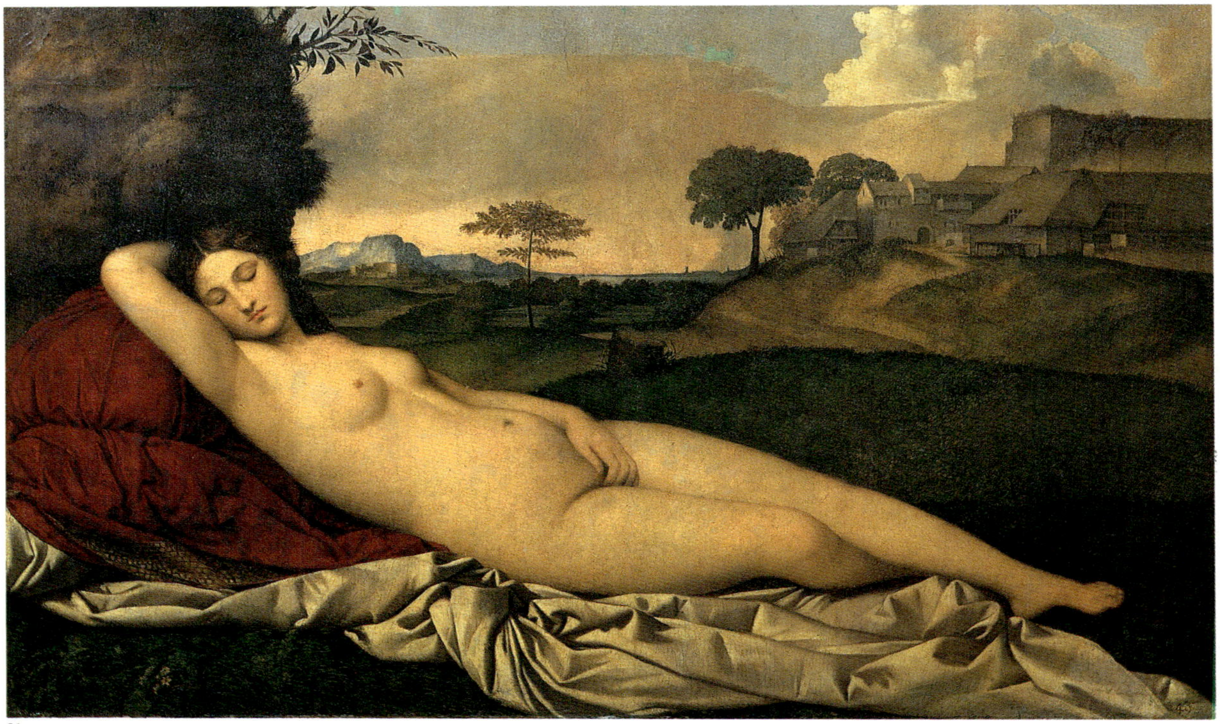

21

21, 22. Sleeping Venus *(the* Dresden Venus*), c.1510, canvas, 108 x 175 cm. Gemäldegalerie, Dresden.*
This is the first example of a genre which was destined to meet with great success in sixteenth century Venetian painting, above all thanks to Titian, who in all probability brought to completion the work, which Giorgione had left unfinished. The body of the naked girl seems to reflect the gentle curves of the hills, as she lies stretched out in the soft peaceful light of the countryside. The image, far from trying to suggest the sensuality of Venus, seems rather to display the contemplative spirit which Giorgione often expressed before beautiful women and nature.

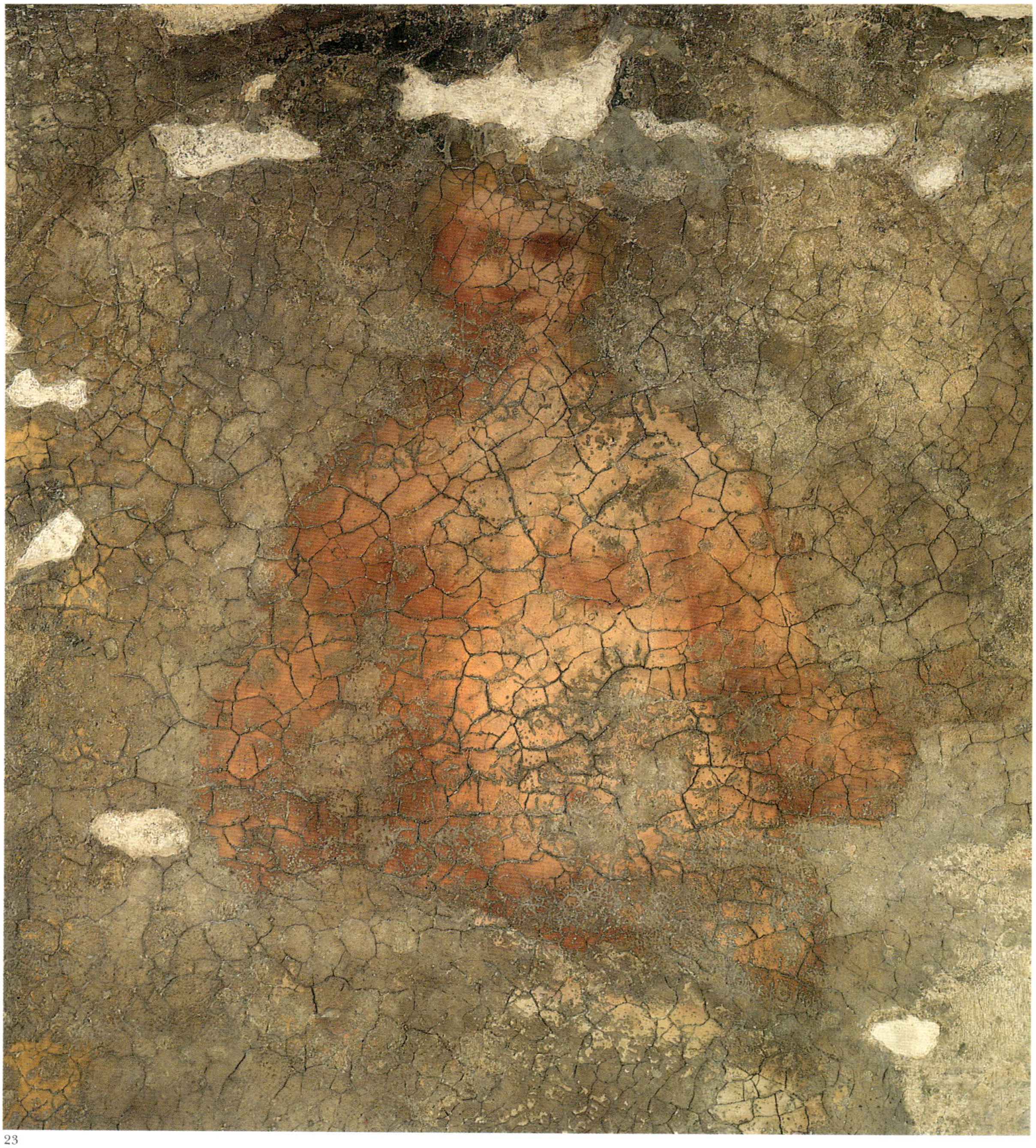

23

23. Nude of a Young Woman,
c. 1508, fresco, 250 x 140 cm.
Gallerie dell'Accademia, Venice.

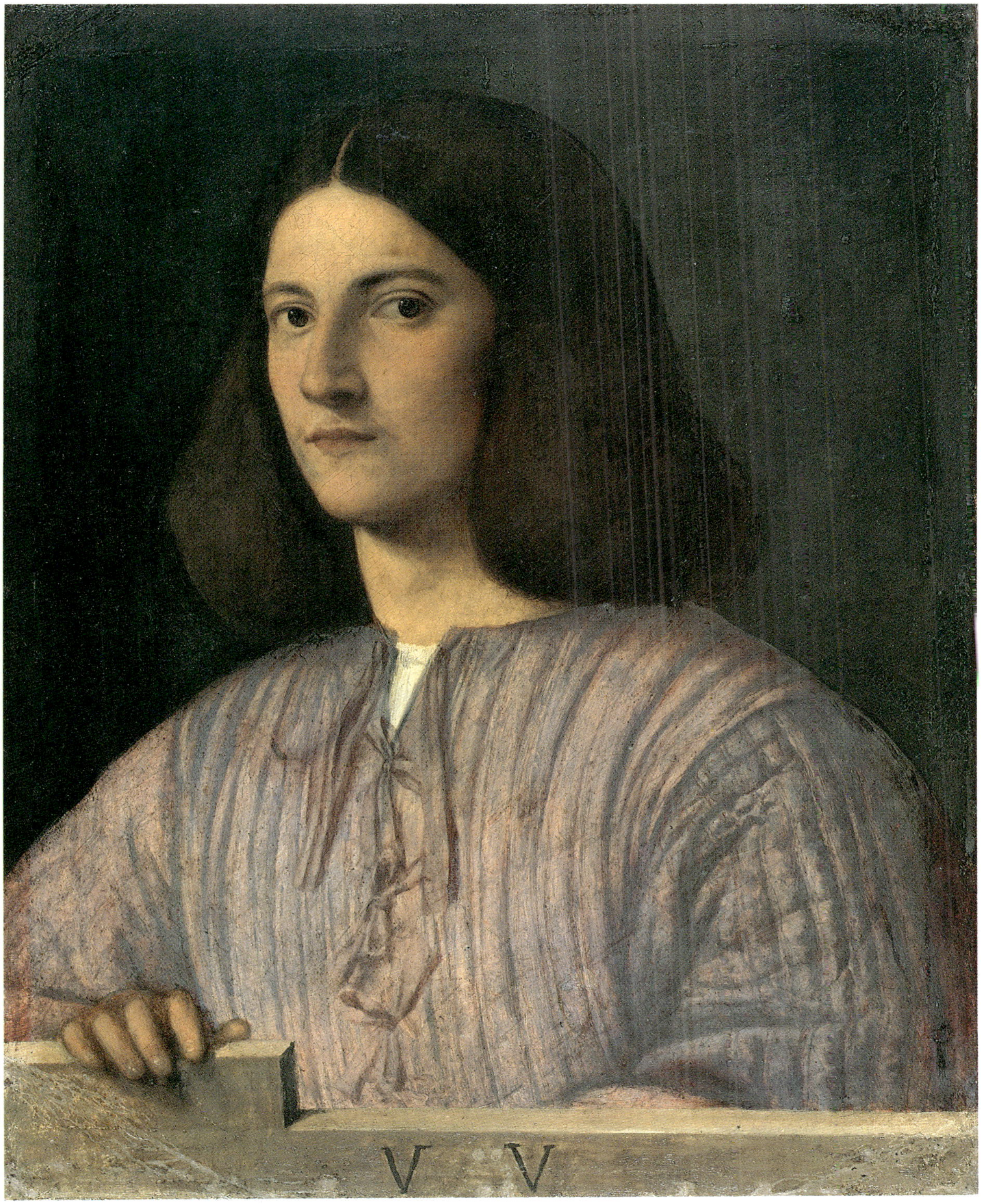

24

24. Portrait of a Young Man (Giustiniani Portrait)*, c. 1510, canvas, 58 x 46 cm. Staatliche Museen, Berlin.*
In the still very uncertain area of Giorgione's portraiture, this is one of the paintings about which there is the greatest degree of consensus among scholars. Among the reasons for this is the subtle psychological treatment, tinged with melancholy, which seems to be the main feature of Giorgione's portraits.

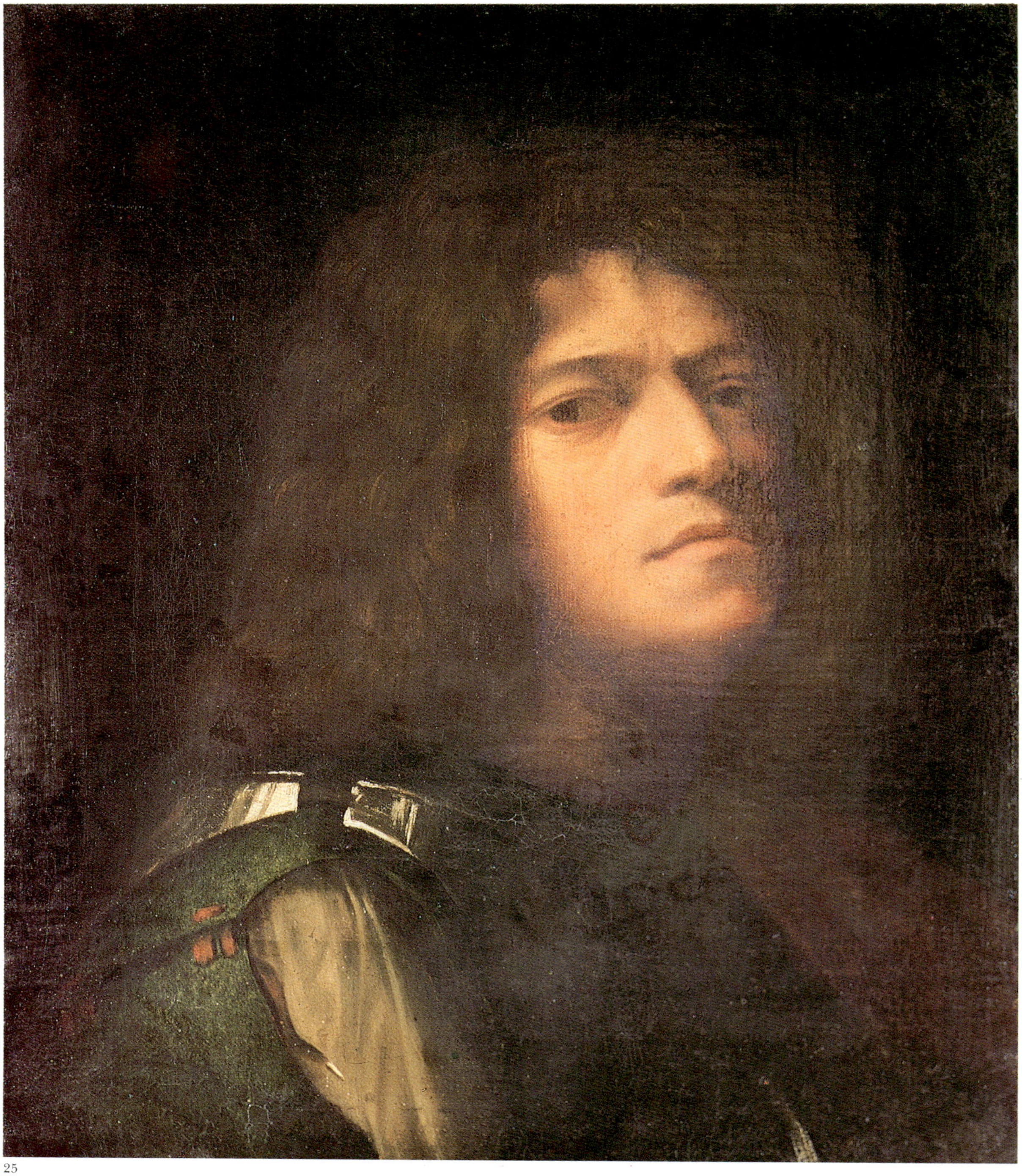

25

25. Self-Portrait as David, *c.1508, canvas, 52 x 43 cm. Herzog Anton Ulrich Museum, Brunswick.*
The painting, which is in a poor condition and from which the lower part is missing, has been recognised as a self-portrait by Giorgione on the basis of old descriptions and prints. Originally the artist portrayed himself as David with Goliath's head.

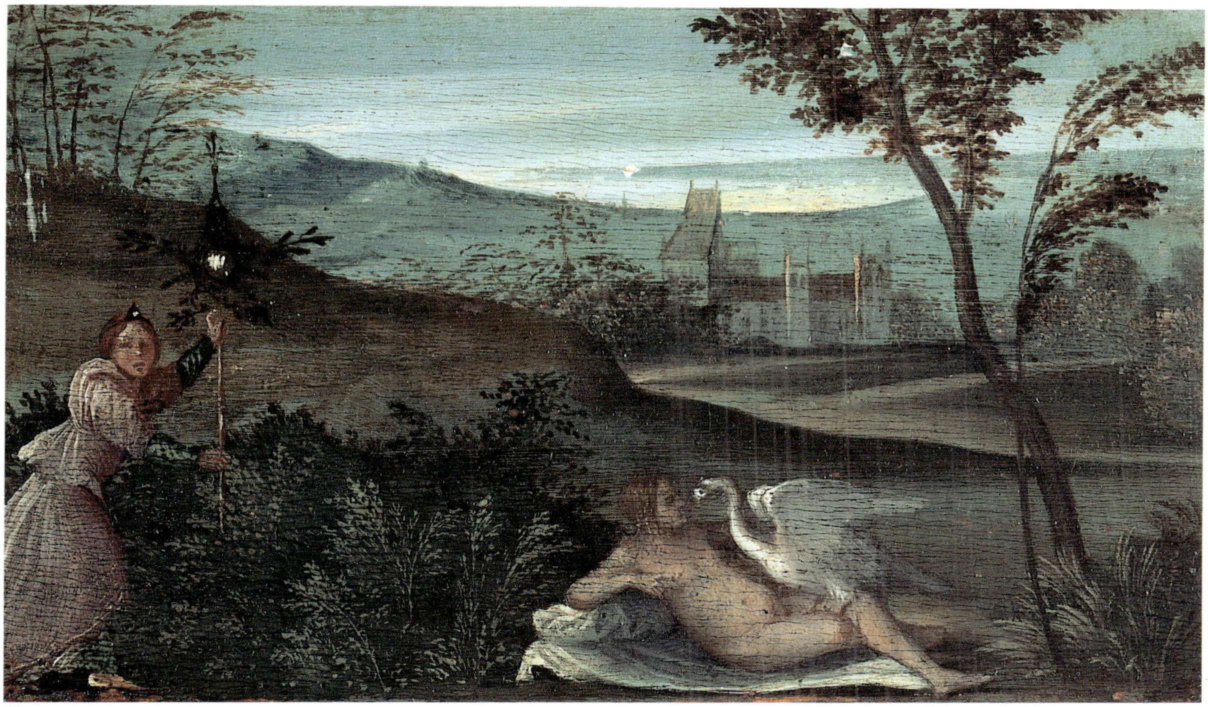

26

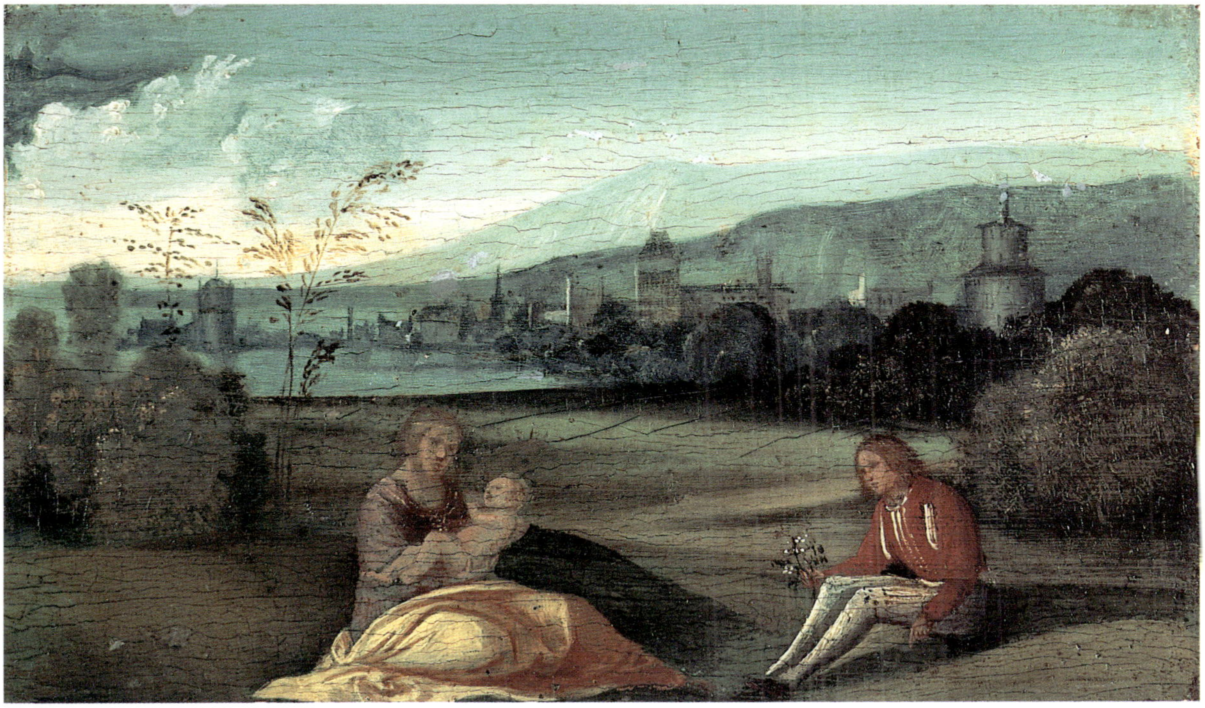

27

26, 27. Leda, *c.1508;* Man, Woman and Child in a Landscape, *c.1508, panels, 12 x 19 cm each. Museo Civico (Legato Emo-Capodilista), Padua.*

The two minute panels originally decorated a piece of furniture, probably a dressing-table. While there are a number of other similar paintings which appear to be the work of the circle of Giorgione, invariably with Arcadian themes, the Padua panels seem to be those which are most likely to be by the artist himself.

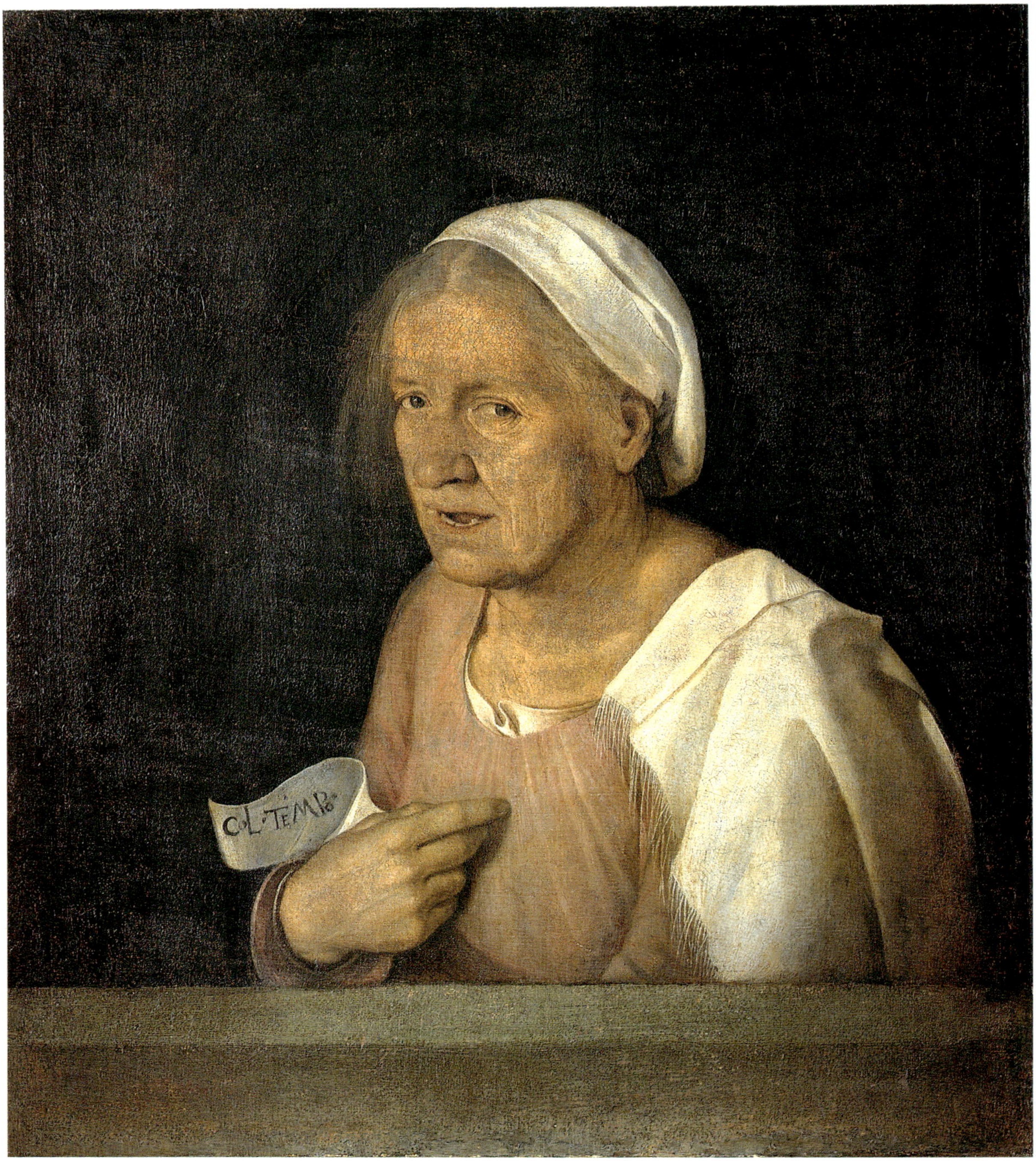

28

28. Portrait of an Old Lady, *1508-1510, canvas, 68 x 59 cm. Gallerie dell'Accademia, Venice. An allegorical portrait, which was painted in the final period of Giorgione's short career, when the artist often expressed feelings of a somewhat melancholy nature. The elderly woman, with her expression and features disfigured by age, holds in her hand a sign with the chilling reminder* col tempo *("with time"), and offers a disenchanted image of the destiny of worldly beauty.*

29

29. Double Portrait, *c.1510, canvas, 80 x 67 cm. Museo di Palazzo Venezia, Rome. The differing quality of the two figures suggests that the painting was executed by two artists, as was often the case in the circle of Giorgione. While the boy in the background is a fairly conventional portrait, the young man in the foreground, seen romantically against the light, is one of the most original inventions of portraiture in the early sixteenth century, even though the attribution to Giorgione is not accepted by all scholars.*

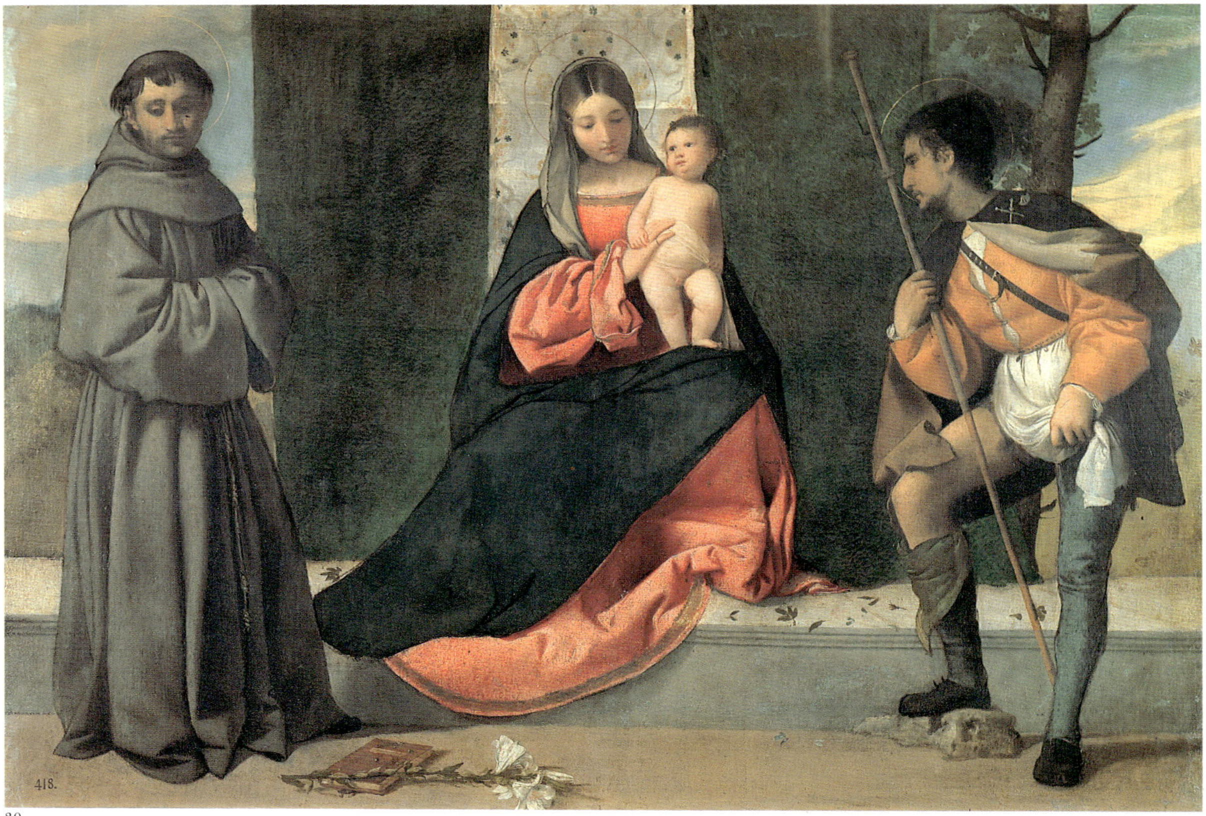

30

30, 31. Giorgione or Titian. Virgin and Child with Saint Anthony and Saint Roch, *c.1510, canvas, 92 x 133 cm. Prado, Madrid. This is a small altarpiece, perhaps of votive origin. The picture was carefully composed to make the best possible use of the shape of the canvas and the colours are unusually vivid. The painting was executed in the period when there was a close relationship between Giorgione and Titian. In this case, too, the attribution is a very controversial issue.*

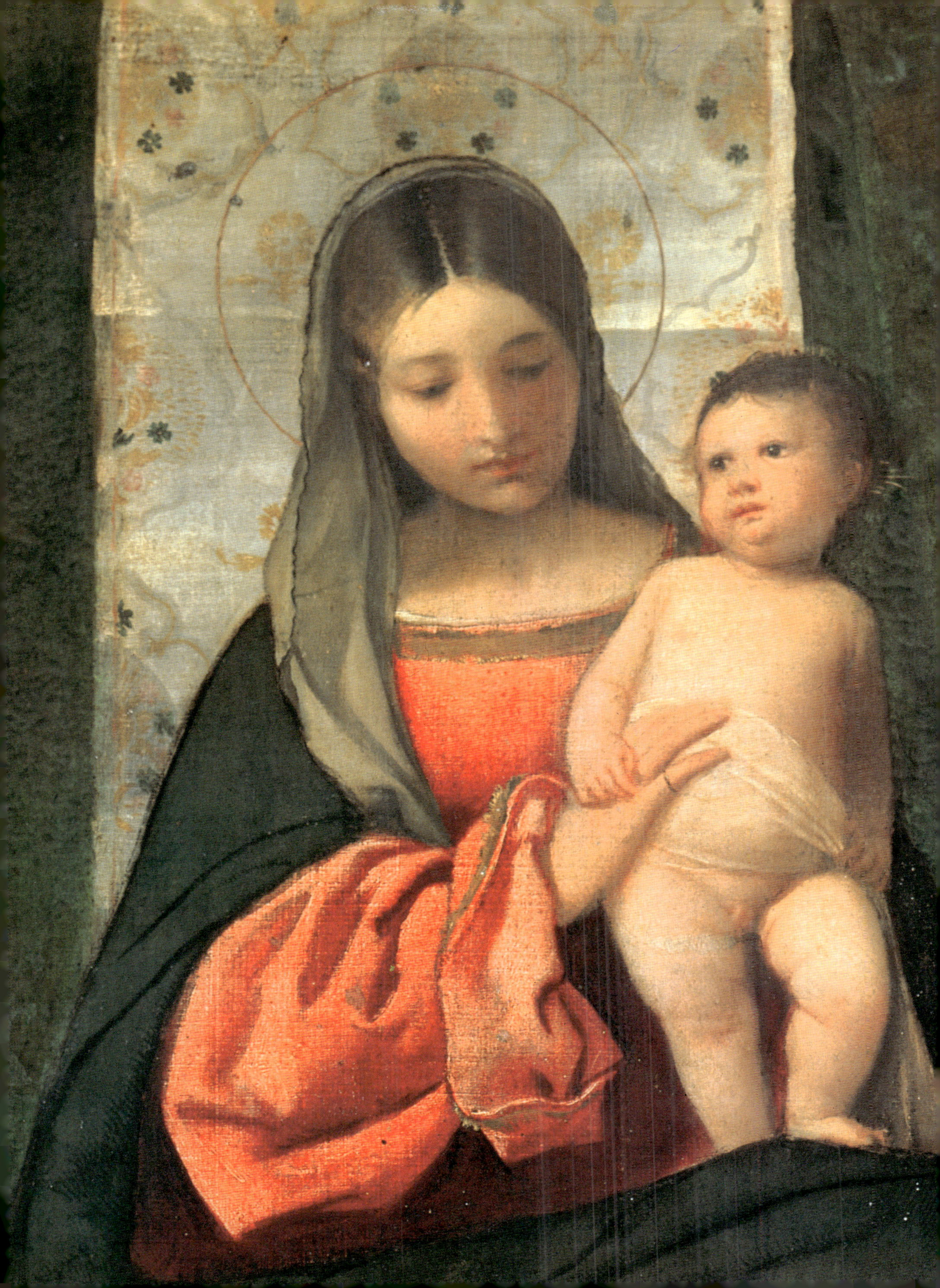

32. Giorgione or Titian, Fête Champêtre, *1510, canvas, 110 x 138 cm. Louvre, Paris. This famous painting, which was an ideal model for the Impressionist painters, is perhaps the most evident case of an unresolved doubt regarding attribution. In fact at the present stage of studies, it is not possible to establish the authorship of the work with absolute certainty. It is, however, a typically Giorgionesque composition because of the harmony between the landscape and the figures, resolved with rhythmical luminosity. Nevertheless, it cannot be ruled out that the painting was completed by Titian, perhaps after the 1510 plague epidemic, which caused Giorgione's untimely death.*

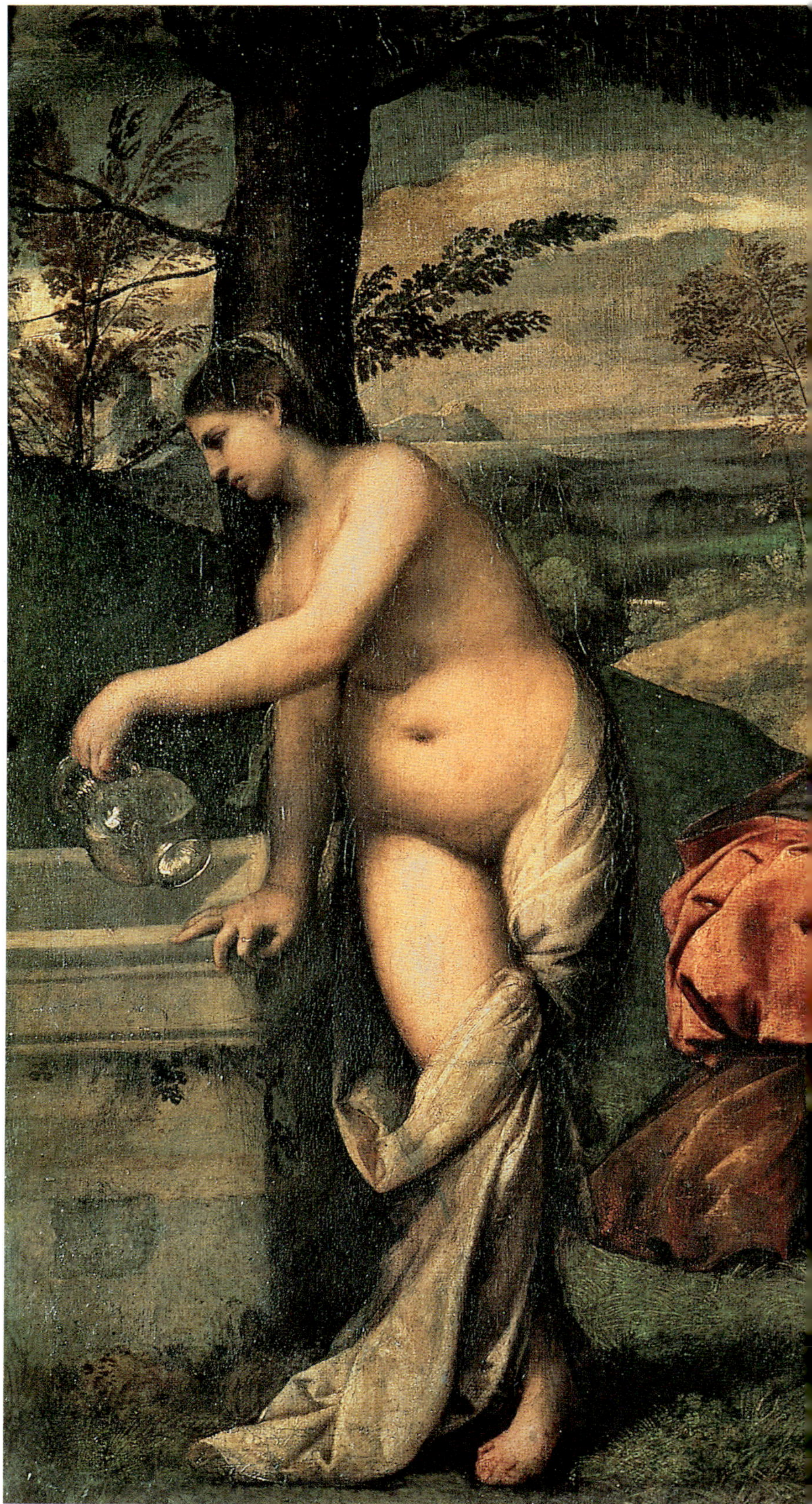

32

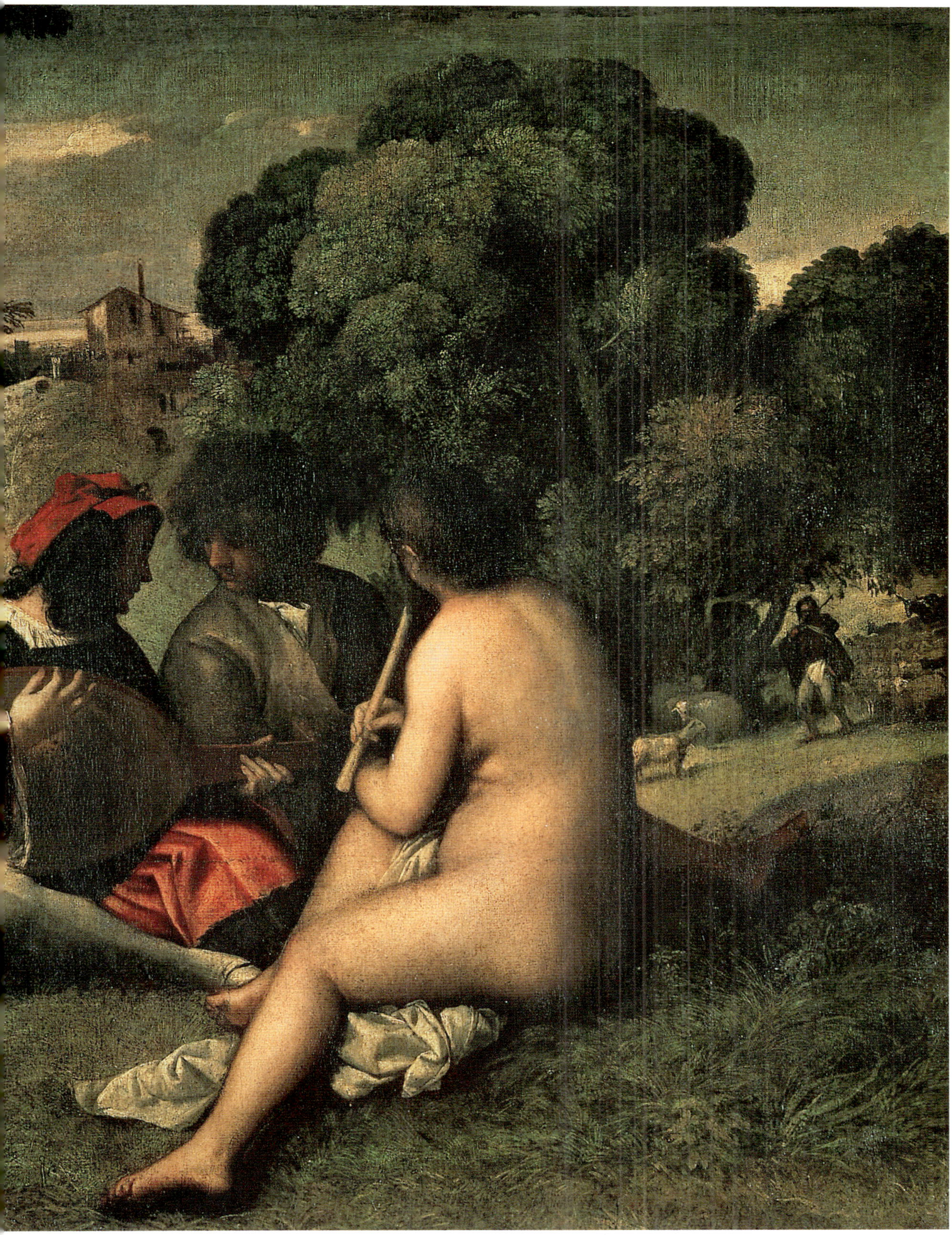

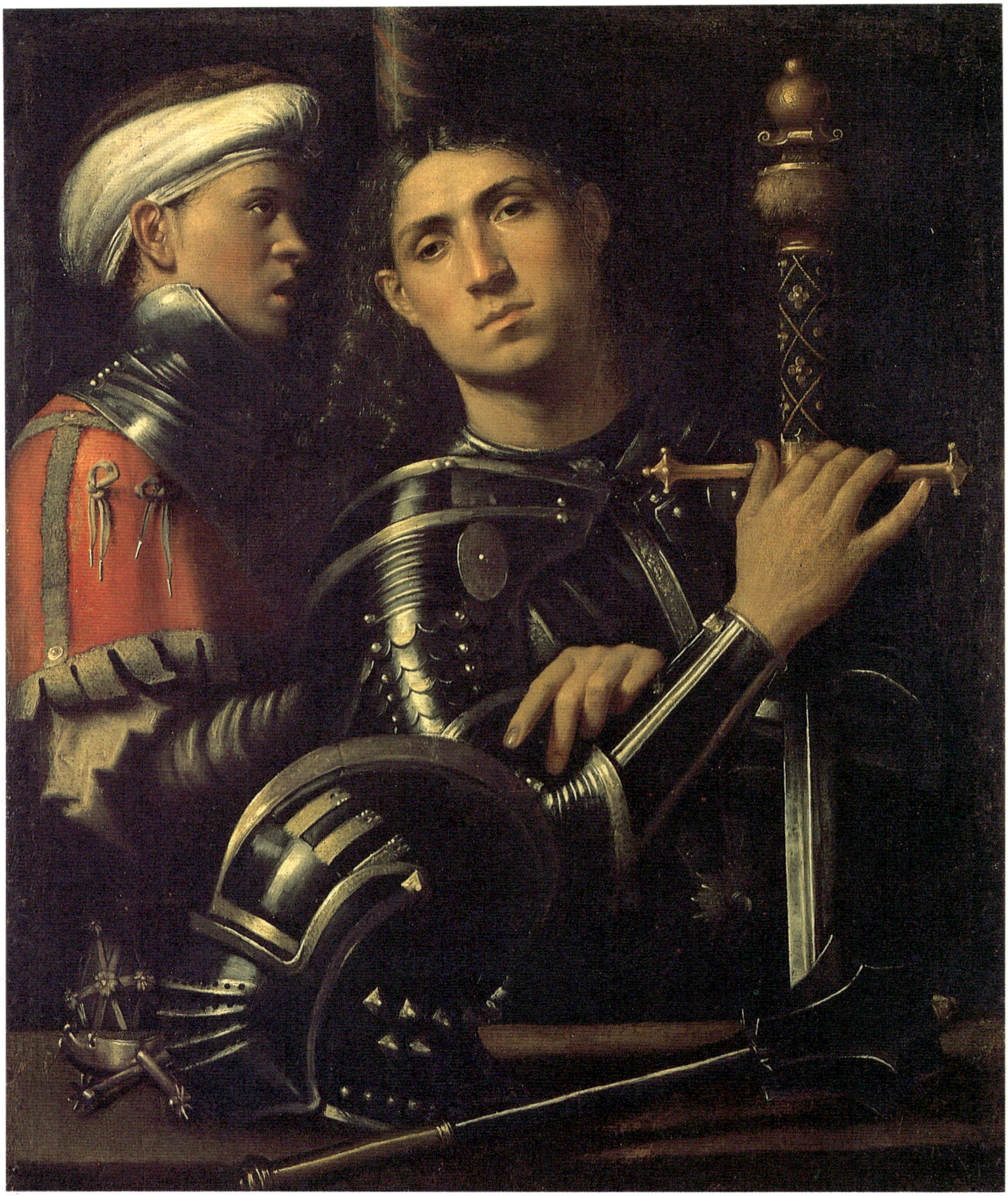

33

33, 34. Gentleman in Armour (Il Gattamelata)*, c.1510, canvas, 80 x 73 cm. Galleria degli Uffizi, Florence.*
Also in this case many scholars do not accept the attribution to Giorgione. On the other hand, the portrait perfectly expresses the artist's poetic vision at the end of his brief career, when his work was increasingly imbued with a spirit of noble melancholy. Indeed, the extremely refined and complex play of the light on the armour can be attributed to the research into reflected light which was typical of Giorgione, as the old sources testify.

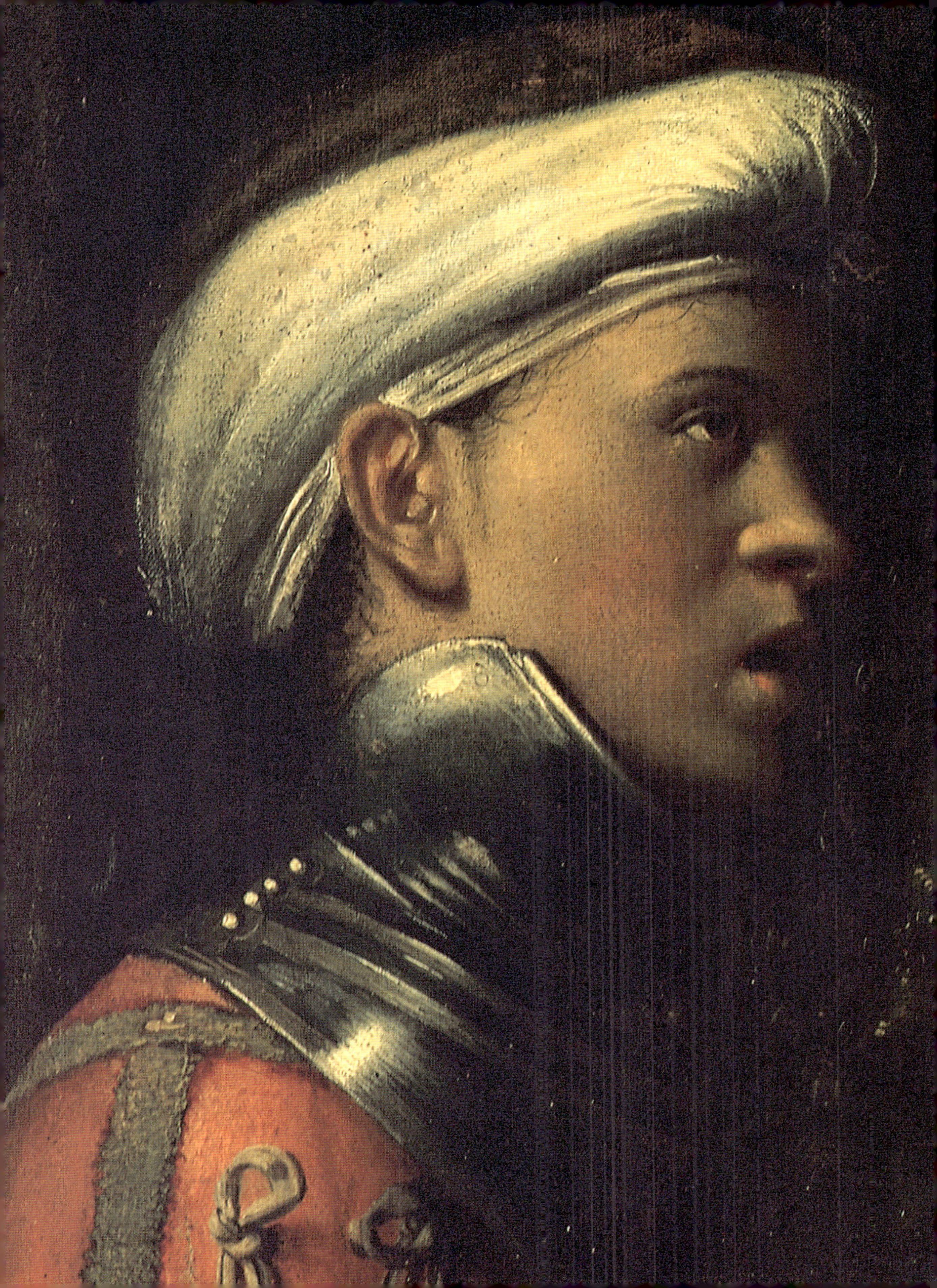

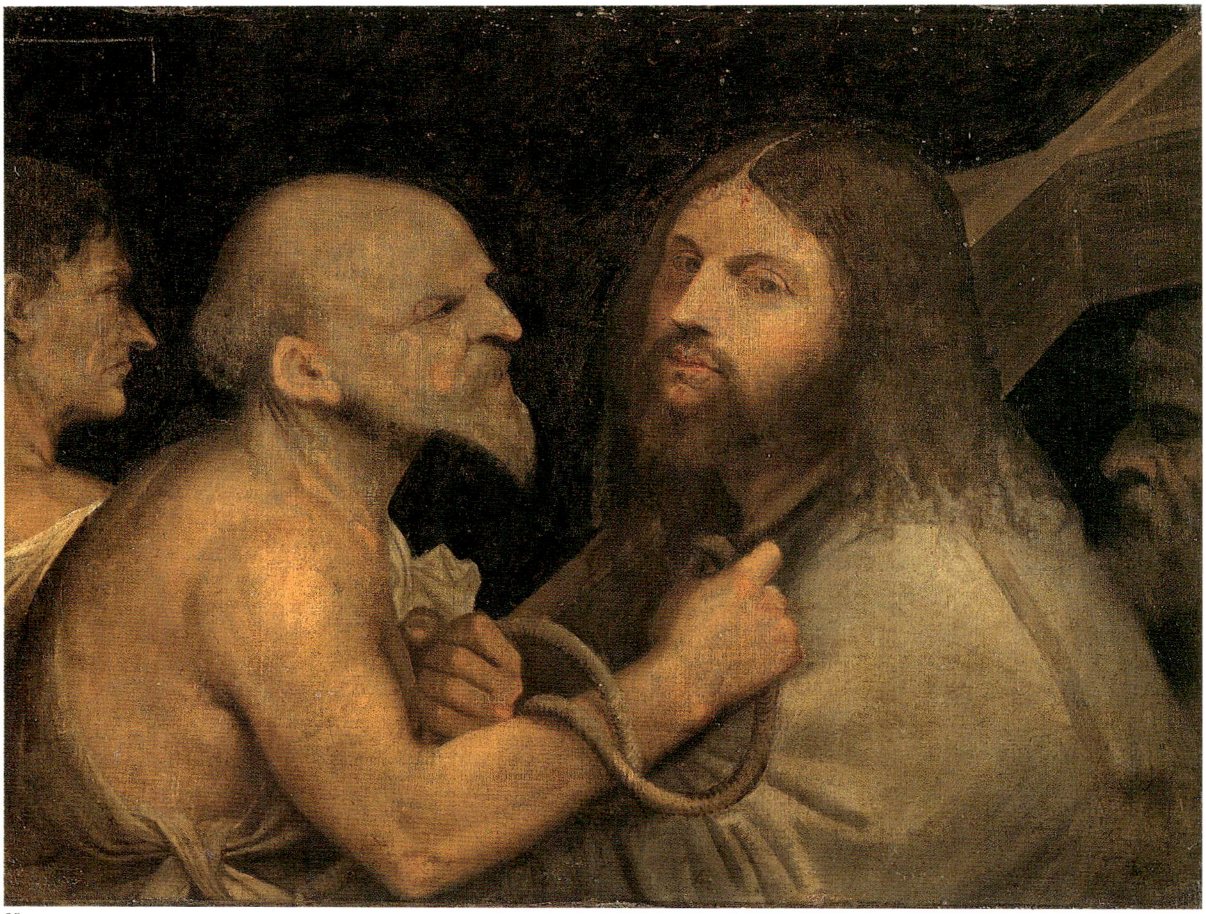

35

35. Giorgione or Titian, Christ Carrying the Cross, *c.1510, canvas, 70 x 100 cm. Scuola Grande di San Rocco, Venice.*
Even the contemporaries were uncertain whether it was a work by Giorgione or Titian. Laden with unusual expressive pathos, for a long period this painting was the object of intense popular devotion, and this is one reason why its state of conservation is so poor.

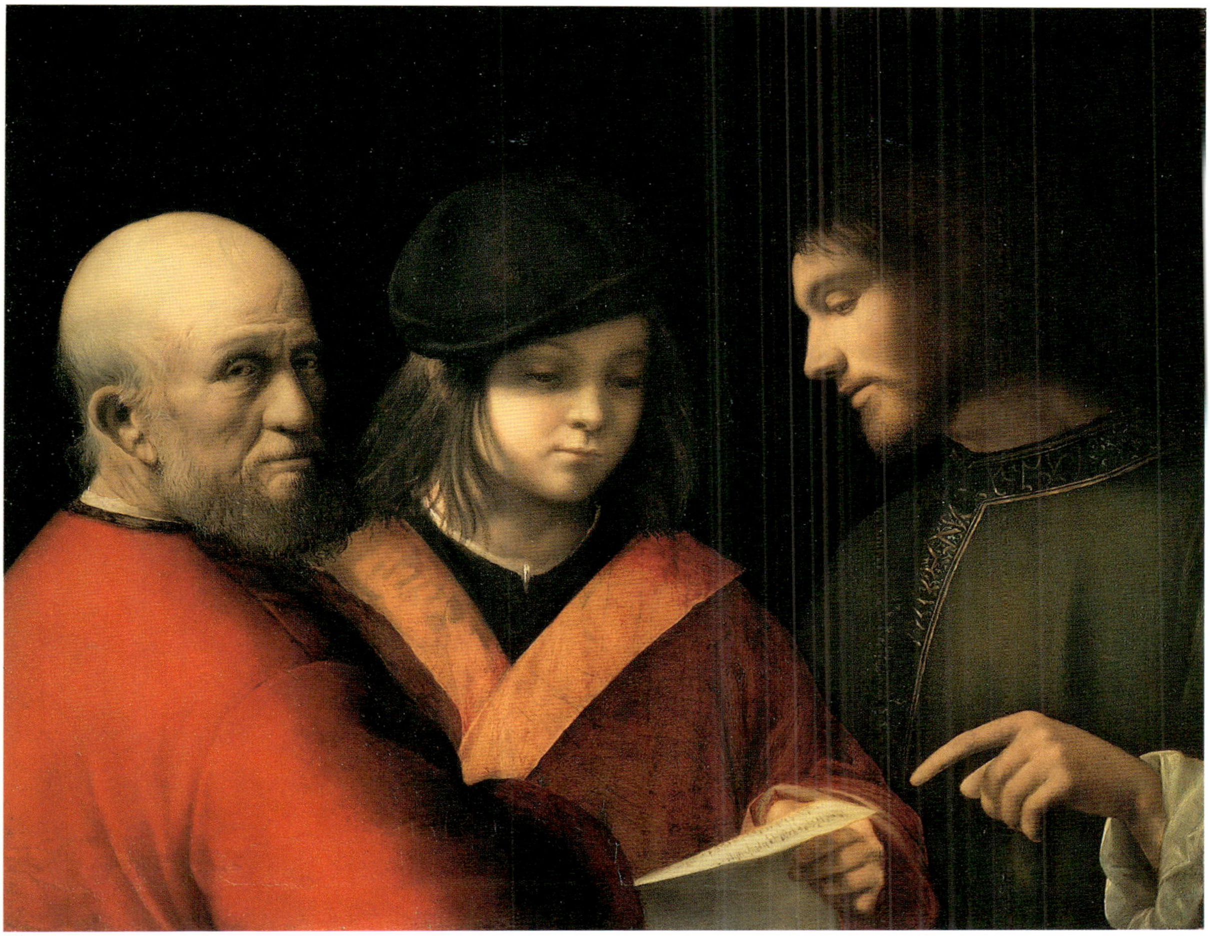

36

36, 37. Three Ages of Man (Concert), *c.1510, canvas, 62 x 77 cm. Galleria Palatina, Palazzo Pitti, Florence.*
The painting is a typical example of the moralising allegories produced by Giorgione and his circle, and it is possible that it was executed by a number of artists. Because of the delicate texture of the light and the atmosphere of calm pensiveness, it can be considered, at least in part, to be one of the last paintings which it is possible to attribute to Giorgione, completed shortly before he died of the plague in the summer of 1510.

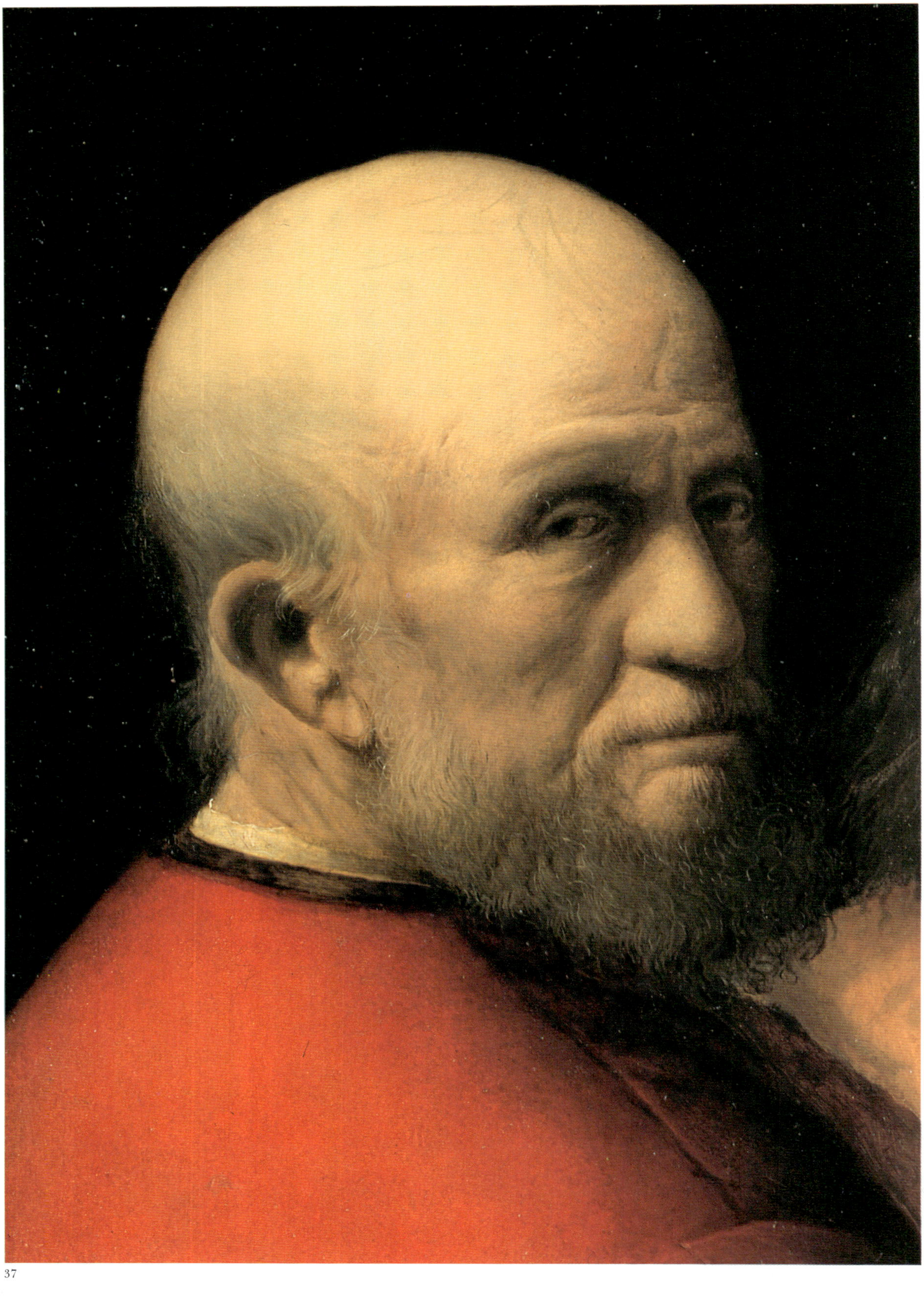

37

Essential Bibliography

C. Volpe, *Giorgione*, Milan 1963.
E. Lombardo Petrobelli, *Giorgione*, Florence 1966.
L'opera completa di Giorgione, edited by P. Zampetti, Milan 1968.
L. Magugliani, *Introduzione a Giorgione e alla pittura veneziana del Rinascimento*, Milan 1970.
S. Settis, La "*Tempesta*" *interpretata. Giorgione, i committenti, il soggetto*, Turin 1978.
Giorgione a Venezia, Milan 1978.
T. Pignatti, *Giorgione. L'opera completa*, Milan 1978.
Giorgione, acts of the conference (Castelfranco Veneto, 1978), Castelfranco Veneto 1979.
S.J. Freedberg, *The Pelican History of Art, Painting in Italy 1500-1600*, Harmondsworth, Middlesex 1979.
Giorgione e la cultura veneta tra '400 e '500, acts of the conference (Rome 1978), Rome 1981.
The Genius of Venice 1500-1600, catalogue of the exhibition, Royal Academy of Art, London 1983.
Frederick Hartt, *History of Italian Renaissance Art*, London 1987.

Photographic Credits
Elemond Archives Milan.
Foto Saporetti, Milan.
Nimatallah/Luisa Ricciarini, Milan.
Photo Service Gruppo Editoriale Fabbri, Milan.
Scala, Florence.

Printed for Arnoldo Mondadori Arte
by Fantonigrafica - Elemond Editori Associati